PRAISE FOR ANGELS DEMONS GHOSTS

"It was very informative in describing the different types of spiritual beings that exist in the spiritual realms. It was very interesting how Virginia talked about the different types of spirit beings and how to respond to each one if contacted."
* Rodney Allgood, motivational speaker and founder of mindSHIFT 360

"I really like the way Virginia talks about the angels and the Archangels and how we can actually contact and meet our Guardian Angels. We can actually receive guidance from our Guardian Angels. She has a great meditation in the book and other exercises to communicate and work with the angels. I would recommend this book if you want to know more about angels, especially the Archangels and their specialties."
* Gloria Bell, author of *Healing Yourself Made Simple*

"I really enjoyed reading Virginia's book. There were interesting stories of her own experiences and other people's experiences. I can relate to some of these experiences and stories. They are similar to what I had. The other information was good because it gave me some information about how the different spiritual beings were different and how they operate. She also talked about how to respond to them if contacted. I enjoyed the meditations and exercises in the book. This book is great for anybody who is interested in spiritual growth and wants to use the protection and spiritual warfare techniques in everyday life."

 * David Armstrong, author of *Messages from the Spirit World: Awakening to Your Soul*

"I enjoyed how many of the chapters in the book had key points at the end of the chapter. It helped me to review the basic protection and spiritual warfare techniques that I want to start using in my everyday life."

 * Brent Scarpo, author of *The Red Balloon*

"I recommend this book to anyone who is interested in contacting and communicating with Guardian Angels, spirit guides, Master teachers, deceased loved ones, and the Archangels. Virginia not only describes the specialties of the Archangels but also has a meditation to contact your Guardian Angel."

 * Adrianne Carlino Gentile, author of *Integrity in the Mirror* and *66 Leaves*

"I really enjoyed Virginia's book because it showed me healing techniques that I can use every day. It also taught me to pay attention to my intuition and gut feelings, especially when I need to make decisions in my life."

 * Grace Fiorre, author of *The Nothing Spirit*

"In *Angels Demons Ghosts*, Virginia assists readers to be able to connect with their Guardian Angels and receive guidance. She also helps people work with the Archangels to clear out and cleanse not only a person's chakras but their aura as well."

* Annnnna, author of *The Omnia Project*

"What amazing real-life encounter stories… They were very interesting and unusual. Anyone who is interested in the paranormal would enjoy this book."

* Bill McCarrick, author of *Are You Hurt or Are You Injured?*

"I enjoyed the section in the book *Angels Demons Ghosts* on the different spiritual warfare techniques, which were presented for people to use on a daily basis to clear out negative energies, spirits, ghosts, and biological entities."

* Lisa Ulshafer, author of *Journey with an Angel*

"This book will bring you meditations and not only protection techniques but also exercises for spiritual cleansing to use in your everyday practical life."

* Mari Rose, author of *Change Your Layers…Change Your Life*

"If you want to know how all the Archangels can help you and about their specialties, Virginia's book will show you how to contact the Archangels and work with them."

* Charmaine Lee, author of *Gardenias Bruise Easily: Giving Silence a Voice—From Abuse to Love*

"If you are curious about angels, spirits, and ghosts, this book will open your mind to what's out there and possible in the paranormal universe."

* Patrick Snow, international best-selling author of *Creating Your Own Destiny* and *The Affluent Entrepreneur*

ANGELS DEMONS GHOSTS

ANGELS DEMONS GHOSTS

HOW TO IDENTIFY AND RESPOND
TO SUPERNATURAL SPIRITS

———

Dr. Virginia Wade

AVIVA
PUBLISHING
New York

ANGELS DEMONS GHOSTS
How to Identify and Respond to Supernatural Spirits
Copyright 2016 Dr. Virginia Wade.
All rights reserved.
Published by:
Aviva Publishing
Lake Placid, NY
(518) 523-1320
www.avivapubs.com

ISBN: 9781943164653
ISBN 10: 1943164657
Library of Congress Control Number: 2016941014
Author Photo: Joseph Donato

Every attempt has been made to properly source all quotes.
Printed in the United States of America.
First Edition

DEDICATION

In memory of my dear friend Victoria Houde. I express my deepest gratitude for her inspiration, emotional support, and belief in my ability to write this book. I dedicate this work to her as an expression of our friendship.

To my good friends David De Broveck, Frank and Diane Goley, Jane Locascio Munson, Crystal Peterson, and Cheryl Comstock, who have been there for support and have encouraged me through the years to go after my dreams.

ACKNOWLEDGMENTS

Patrick Snow deserves all the credit for helping me write this book. Thank you for your direction, encouragement, and expertise.

To all my friends and clients who have come to me for guidance, I thank you for your support and belief in me. I hope you enjoy the book. I express my deepest gratitude.

I would also like to thank and recognize the following people for their encouragement, support, and belief in me: Calvin D. Banyan, Shirley Beverly, Mel Bond, Laverne Bower, Sylvia Brown, Jesus Christ, Jeanette Corwin, Wayne Dyer, Ron Edlinger, Tony Evans, Linda Edner, Bruce Goldberg, Kenneth Hagin, Mark Hankins, Dennis Michael Harness, Louise Hay, Marlys Ilie, T. D. Jakes, Riley Martin, Shakuntala Modi, Shahrokh Mohammadzadeh, George Noory, Joel Osteen, David Quigley, Alan Sampson, Charlie Sampson, Dino Servente, Rose Servente, David Shearin, Chuck Smith, Charles Stanley, Victoria Stitzer, Mae St. Claire, Tony Stubbs, Dick Sutphen, Brian Tracy, Coreen Vanwie, Doreen Virtue, Marcel Vogel, Paramahansa Yogananda, Ethel Wade, Dael Walker, and Maxine White.

CONTENTS

IDENTIFYING AND RESPONDING TO ANGELS, DECEASED LOVED ONES, AND GHOSTS

———◆———

Can you imagine driving to the funeral of a loved one and all of a sudden hearing his or her voice speak loudly in your mind? Not believing what you just heard, you would certainly ask yourself whether you might be going crazy.

You tell yourself, "No, I could not have just heard that!" Then the voice is there again, and you look over to see your loved one sitting in the passenger seat next to you—in spirit form. You realize it must be true; this is really happening. You believe!

This really did happen to me, and it could happen to you. I was in shock from the death and was very skeptical at first. Until it happened to me, I would not have believed such things were possible. I understand if you feel skeptical about that story or about seeing a ghost. I felt the same way until my deceased father appeared to me and spoke into my mind that day. As skeptical as I was at the time, it was actually happening. I talked to him for one and a half hours as I drove to Phoenix, Arizona, to catch a flight to California for the funeral.

This book will help you to be able to tell the difference between angels, demons, ghosts, spirit guides, deceased loved ones, and biological entities. You will learn how to identify each type of visitor and how to respond to each if contacted. You will be able to contact and connect with your Guardian Angel and the Archangels to receive divine guidance for your everyday life. This book will also help you discriminate between true divine guidance and false guidance when you receive messages. The Archangels and their specialties will help you in different areas of your life. The practical protection exercises and angelic meditations within this book will help you to activate your angels. You will discover how angels can bring you messages and signs and communicate with you. God's angels can improve your life in many ways.

This book includes real-life encounters with spirits and ghosts that others and I have had. It will help you understand how to connect with your deceased loved ones and how to receive messages from them. You will then learn how you can send them into the light. Practicing protection techniques and spiritual warfare exercises with Jesus Christ, Archangel Michael, Saint Germain, and the Angelic Host will benefit you greatly. You will be able to use the tools of Archangel Michael for spiritual warfare, for dealing with difficult people, and for cleansing your aura and chakras. You will find easy techniques you can use to remove negative energies, spirit attachments, and ghosts from your aura and your home. This book will also help you experience the healing techniques of the Archangels.

Now I will tell you about myself. In 1979, I completed a bachelor's degree at San Jose State University in art and health education. I learned about meditation in my church. I took a training session on releasing spirits and ghosts and learned how to send deceased loved ones into the light. In 1992, I moved to Sedona, Arizona, and worked as a medical assistant. I started feeling the pain of my patients. I became empathic. I opened up psychically and started encountering different other-dimensional spirits. I learned how to identify and respond to each one as I had these different experiences. When the family practice I was working for closed for restructuring in 1998, I moved to Las Vegas, Nevada. In 2005, I took classes at the University of Metaphysics, now called the University of Sedona, and received a doctorate degree in metaphysics. I completed a hypnotherapy/NLP and Timeline Therapy practitioner training with Tad James in 2007, receiving certificates in all three. This enabled me to do Past Life Regressions, Timeline Therapy, and Hypnotherapy.

In 2010, I branched out with further training in pain management techniques that use visualization and metaphors in hypnotherapy. I also learned how to release spirits and ghosts from homes, individuals, and work-related environments. I send them into the light or to the second dimension through the help of Archangel Michael and Jesus Christ's name. I clear haunted houses in Jesus Christ name after discovering why the ghosts are there and what they want. I can see into other dimensions and into the spiritual realms. As I send ghosts into the light,

I can actually see them ascending, so I know when they have reached the light. My own deceased loved ones have returned to me for help to reach the light after they have died.

I became aware of the Archangels at work when a customer came in and told me she saw Archangel Michael working with me. This inspired me to do research and learn more about Archangel Michael. I started working with Archangel Michael and Archangel Raphael. These Archangels now assist me as I call on them and give them permission to help. They have shown me the tools they use in spiritual warfare, for cleansing the aura, and for healing.

I was in a work situation in 2012 where I had to use these spiritual warfare tools to survive at my job. The job was very abusive. Using the white light, the violet flame, Archangel Michael's blue light of protection, and Jesus Christ name and blood, I survived at the job for nine months. I now know God placed me in that situation so I could practice the spiritual warfare techniques I had learned up to that point. Instead of letting myself become a victim, I used those tools to take control of my life. Now I am here to share these techniques with you.

The Spirit Realms are Real

It is normal to question whether what is coming into your mind as your imagination or a communication from your Guardian Angel or deceased loved one. It is okay at first to be fearful about the spiritual realms. I will show you everything you need to know about protection techniques and safe ways to communicate with your Guardian Angel or deceased loved one. Angels do exist, and your deceased loved one is ready to talk to you. Your Guardian Angel is watching over you, protecting you, and sending you love. Just acknowledge his or her presence, and give your permission for the angel to communicate with you.

In this book, I will give you easy exercises and meditations to help you contact your angels and deceased loved ones. You will feel safe and protected as I guide you into the spiritual realms. I will give you clear instructions on techniques for how to identify and respond to angels, ghosts, spirit guides, deceased loved ones, and biological entities. When you start opening up, it is natural to become afraid. This book will explain protection techniques. When spirits start appearing to you, you will know how to identify and respond to them. As you become more sensitive and psychically open, receiving spirit communications in your mind, you will gradually build confidence and know how to respond. You will be able to use the techniques presented here to clear out all negative spirits from your home and your life.

It is equally important, though, to know and become aware of the symptoms of a psychic attack. I will give you techniques to neutralize any psychic attack and to clear out your aura of negative thought forms, spirit attachments, and negative cords between other people and yourself. I will also give you techniques on how to prevent energy vampires from draining your energy. With the assistance of the Archangels, your aura will be cleared out, strengthened, and sealed.

You may not realize that the root of all physical problems begin in the spiritual realms and are created by spirits. Once you know how to respond to spirits and to send them away through spiritual warfare techniques, healing becomes possible. You can approach physical problems from a spiritual standpoint through spiritual warfare tools. Then you can be in control of your health instead of feeling like a victim. Let me help you with any questions you may have concerning spiritual warfare, healing, and working with the angels.

Are you ready to begin your journey to discover what messages and guidance your Guardian Angel and your deceased loved ones want to give you? If so, let us go explore the spiritual realms. I will guide you. Come join me. We will take this journey together.

Dr. Virginia Wade

PART I

UNDERSTANDING THE ANGELIC REALMS

CHAPTER 1

DISCOVERING THE DIFFERENT TYPES OF ANGELS

———

Bless the Lord, ye his angels that excel
in strength, that do his commandments,
hearkening unto the voice of his word.

—Psalm *103:20 KJV*

In this chapter, we are going to be covering the different types of angels and their purposes. Each type has a particular purpose assigned by the Almighty God, the Creator.

Who are the Angels?

Throughout time, people have always wondered if angels are real or just a figment of the imagination. The Bible points to the existence of angels. Do you realize that there are many types of angels?

When people think about angels, they usually think about a Guardian Angel or the Archangels. There are many different types of angels, however, and each serves a different purpose. One way God communicates with us is through His angels. God uses angels to bring messages to us according to His will. He has also created different types of angels for different purposes. This book focuses mainly on the Guardian Angel and the Archangels. These angels work with human beings and bring us messages from God.

Angels are spiritual beings who have never incarnated in a human body. They are immortal. There are only two exceptions to this rule: Enoch became Metatron when he ascended up into the spirit, and Elijah became Sandalphon when he ascended up in the spirit by a whirlwind. Angels are here to provide protection, healing, and divine guidance. God sends angels to encourage us to fulfill our purpose according to God's will. Angels are neither male nor female. They appear to us as male or female so we can identify them as such and relate to them. Each angel has its own specialty in a certain area of life. In the book *Angels,* Billy Graham explains: "Angels are created spirit beings who can become visible when necessary." What he is saying, I believe, is that when you need help, an angel can appear in a human form or become visible to you to give you a message.

The Categories of Angels

1. The Seraphim praise God continually in God's presence. They send us love and light. They have six wings: two wings covering their faces, two wings covering their feet, and two wings for flying.

2. The Cherubim have double wings and reveal God's love and glory while continually praising God. They know about the secret knowledge of God.
3. The Thrones bring peace and are in charge of the manifestation process on earth. They are in charge of God's justice.
4. The Dominions organize the angels under God's will and direction.
5. The Virtues control nature and protect the environment, keeping it in harmony. They are in control of the seasons and the planets and bring blessings and miracles to earth.
6. The Powers work against evil spirits on the earth and clear out negativity. Then they restore the good on earth. They guard and protect the portals between the other side and the physical world.
7. The Principalities are spiritual forces that are ready to do spiritual warfare when needed. The two types of principalities are the angels of God and the demons of Satan.
8. The Archangels are messengers from God to humans and work with us by bringing messages to us. These Archangels have different specialties that cover different aspects of life. They assist us and bring messages to our Guardian Angels, who in turn relay the messages to us. A unique color flame is associated with each Archangel.
9. The angels deliver our prayers up to God and help us as we ask and give permission for them to do so.

10. Guardian Angels watch over us and protect us throughout our whole life. They take our prayers to the Archangels, who then take them to God. These Guardian Angels can continually give us guidance so that we can fulfill our purpose in life.

First Contact with an Archangel

Do the Archangels work with us? I was at work one day, and a customer came into the store. She told me she saw Archangel Michael working with me and around me, protecting me at work! I had no idea until she told me. She mentioned that she was a psychic, and could see into other dimensions. This led me to do research about Archangel Michael, so I could communicate and work with him. I believe now that God sent that customer into the store to let me know that Archangel Michael was trying to communicate with me and to prepare me for my spiritual task ahead. After that day, I realized I could talk to Archangel Michael and give him permission to protect me. Years later, I am now working with Archangel Michael on a daily basis.

Meeting an Angel

You might wonder whether an angel can manifest as a human. One day, I was in a bookstore. I decided to go up a spiral staircase to reach the metaphysical section. The stairs were very old, and as I walked up, they made a lot of noise. The landing at the top was a very small balcony, about eight feet long. There was not much room to walk along the bookshelves. I was the only one up there. I looked over the balcony at the other customers below for a moment, and then I turned back around and started looking at the books. All of a sudden, a person was standing next to me. It shocked me because I did not hear anybody coming up the stairs. It was very quiet in the bookstore. It was a young man. He told me to start writing a journal and that I would be good at writing. I was still trying to figure out how he got up the stairs without making any noise, so I turned back to browsing the bookshelves while I thought about it. Then he was suddenly gone. I thought that was impossible. I had not heard him going down the stairs either and it would have taken him at least a few seconds to walk down about twenty noisy, twisty stairs. He was just instantly gone. Then I realized he must have been an angel. I took his message to heart and started a journal within the next few days.

Seeing my Guardian Angel

We all have Guardian Angels. Some of us even have more than one Guardian Angel.

One day in 1982, I walked into my living room and I noticed a medium-blue light glowing along the draperies in my living room. The light was very tall and so dense it blocked me from being able to see the fabric behind it. This light must have been at least seven feet tall and three feet wide. I could not figure out what it was—I certainly had no idea it could have been my Guardian Angel. Months later, a friend of mine who was psychic told me that my Guardian Angel was very tall, blue and big. Only then did I realize what I had seen. It had to have been my Guardian Angel. Have you ever wondered what your Guardian Angel looks like?

Touched by An Angel

"I was preparing to give a talk at church one time, and I was afraid that the information I was going to present would not be accepted by the attendees. I was feeling upset about it. All of a sudden, I felt a warm feeling come over me and I felt angelic arms around me. Then I received a telepathic message that everything would be okay. I was startled, so I moved my body. The presence stepped away. Everything did turn out well. I was reminded that good always happens." (Lori)

How would you ask your Guardian Angel to help you? Make a list of questions you would ask your Guardian Angel.

1. _____

2. _____

3. _____

4. _____

5. _____

CHAPTER 2

PREPARING TO CONTACT AND COMMUNICATE WITH ANGELS

———

I will say of the Lord, He is my refuge and
my fortress: my God; in him will I trust.

—PSALMS *91:2 KJV*

In the last chapter, we talked about the different types
of angels. They serve God and bring messages and guidance to us. In this chapter, we are going to be talking
about protection techniques. How do you prepare to contact and communicate with angels? We are going to learn
not only how to protect ourselves with colored lights but
also how to run energy through our body and to ground
it. This stabilizes our energy field so we are able to function better on this physical plane.

Placing Protection Around Us

How do you protect yourself before contacting an angel?
Do you wonder why you need protection, or from what?
What are the protection techniques?

I am here to explain protection techniques. Once you place protection around yourself, you will have protection from negative energies that come at you from all directions every day.

A Simple Protection Exercise

Visualize the white light of the Holy Spirit coming down to the top of your head, at the crown chakra, and flowing down through you until it is underneath your feet. Then visualize the white light of the Holy Spirit spreading out into a bubble around you and your aura protecting you. Now visualize a purple light around the white light. Next, visualize a blue light over that purple light. These concentric rings of light protect you against all negativity. The white light protects you on a physical level. The purple light protects you on a spiritual level. The blue light is the protection of Archangel Michael all around you. Then visualize a green light of healing and protection around you to prevent psychic attack. How do you feel after completing this exercise?

As you go through your day, ask that your aura be veiled so it does not irritate anybody. Your light could be very strong—strong enough to rub others the wrong way.

Grounding and Running Energy Exercise

Visualize a copper energy coming up from the earth, into your feet. Then if you are a woman, visualize it moving up your legs to your pelvic area. If you are a man, visualize this copper energy coming up through your feet, and then up your legs to the base of your spine. Now visualize a shiny copper cord extending from your pelvic area if you are a woman or from the base of your spine if you are a man—down into the center of the Earth. Anchor it there. Continue to visualize this copper earth energy coming up through your feet, up your legs, up to your pelvic area or the base of your spine.

Now visualize a silver-white light coming down at the top of your head, down your back channels, down into the pelvic area or the base of the spine, and mixing with the copper earth energy. Then draw it up the front channels and out the top of your head, like a fountain. Continue visualizing this mixing for about five to ten minutes, concentrating on drawing the energy along your channels.

Next, visualize the white light, the purple light and the blue light of protection again. This is called "running" energy. When you drop down the cord into the center of the Earth and attach it there, it is called "grounding." Grounding is necessary for bringing spiritual consciousness into the physical body and for stabilizing your energy. Grounding enables you to function on the physical plane. In the morning, I recommend that you first ground and run energy, then protect yourself with the white light, purple light, and the blue light.

What I Do Every Morning

How can you prepare to contact and communicate with angels? When I wake up in the morning, I first say hello to the angels and to God, the Holy Spirit, and Jesus Christ. I give God the glory and praise the name of Jesus Christ. I then plead the blood of Jesus Christ over my mind, my heart, and my body. I visualize the white light around me and add the purple light and the blue light for protection. I ground myself by visualizing a copper cord from my pelvic area to anchor me to the center of the Earth.

Then I quiet myself. I begin to meditate and give permission for my Guardian Angel to speak and bring me the guidance I will need for that day. I usually ask, "What am I to do today?" I listen to what he has to say. Usually my Guardian Angel will speak directly into my mind with an answer to that question. I thank my Guardian Angel for his guidance and finish my meditation and prayers.

Next, I call on Archangel Michael and give him permission to come and protect me throughout my day. After that, I ask the Holy Spirit to place me at the right place at the right time to allow me to connect with the right people, according to God's will. I also ask the Holy Spirit to lead me into all truth and to what I am supposed to be doing according to my purpose in life. I call on Archangel Raphael to restore my body to health with his emerald-green light of healing. I also ask him to seal up any tears, cracks, or holes in my aura. I begin saying my mantras.

After that, I feel ready to start my day. If I have time, I will ask Archangel Michael and Archangel Raphael to clear out my chakras and cut me free from all negative thought forms within my aura. I give thanks and go about my day.

Additional Basic Protection Techniques

* Build up your aura with meditation and deep breathing, and visualize a blue-green light throughout your aura.

- Call on the angels to go before you and protect you throughout the day. Be sure to give them permission to do so, and thank them for their services.
- Speak out the promises of the word of God. Pray throughout the day, and acknowledge that angels are all around you.
- Know that white light goes before you, dissolving all negativity.
- Have empathy for others
- Focus on the positive, not on the negative.
- Surround yourself with positive people, and free yourself from complaining people.
- Set boundaries with others to make time to nurture yourself.

What are some of your own protection techniques that you will use today? Make a list, add it to the techniques above, and reference it every day.

1. _____
2. _____
3. _____
4. _____
5. _____

CHAPTER 3

HEARING FROM YOUR GUARDIAN ANGEL

—————

*For he shall give his angels charge over
thee, to keep thee in all thy ways.*

—PSALMS *91:11 KJV*

Jesus said, *"take heed that ye despise not one of these little
ones; for I say unto you, That in heaven their angels do always
behold the face of my Father which is in heaven"* (Matthew
18:10 KJV). I believe he was referring to Guardian
Angels.

In the last chapter, we talked about protection techniques and grounding. In this chapter, we will talk about
how to contact and hear from your Guardian Angel. You
will learn more about your own Guardian Angel.

How Your Guardian Angel Works with You

Who is your Guardian Angel? How can he help you?
Would you like to contact and talk with your Guardian

Angel? What is his purpose in your life? How does he work with you?

Your Guardian Angel is a spiritual, supernatural being who has never been born in a human body. Guardian Angels are therefore not female or male, but will appear in whatever form they know will help us best relate to them. This angel is your personal angel, assigned only to you sent by God to stay with you through your whole life. He will make sure that you fulfill your purpose on Earth according to God's will. He will bring down his presence and love upon you, to comfort you. He receives his guidance from the Archangels and brings it to you. Your Guardian Angel is near you all the time. Your Guardian Angel is here to protect you, watch over you, and guide you into what you are supposed to be doing to serve and help others.

Joanne Brocas affirms these statements in her book, *The Power of Angels*: "The initial way you go about asking your Guardian Angel for help is to simply form and hold a strong mental intention to connect with your Guardian Angel. Remember; energy follows thought, which creates a spiritual link directly to your Guardian Angel."

I feel she is correct in mentioning the importance of forming a strong mental intention to connect with your Guardian Angel. I also believe, since we have free will, we must give our Guardian Angel permission to bring us guidance, speak into our minds, and advise us. When you receive guidance and good ideas, it is usually due to a Guardian Angel. The Guardian Angel will direct you into doing what you are supposed to be doing, and give you signs showing you that he or she is around you and helping you.

Talk to your Guardian Angel as you would to any other person. In an emergency, the Guardian Angel will come to your rescue. You may have more than one Guardian Angel. These angels will not interfere with your free will or your choices. If you start going off in a wrong direction and your actions prevent you from fulfilling your real purpose in life, the angels will bring you back through wake-up calls. A wake-up call is a negative event or a health crisis. It is usually something serious enough to slow you down or stop you, so that you will reevaluate the direction you are going in life. Personally, I will usually pull a muscle when a change of direction is coming. The angels will show you signs to get your attention, and show you changes that are coming up for you. Your Guardian Angel can do small, positive things to keep you on track, like remind you to take your vitamins or your medicine, or remind you if you forget things. The angel can instruct you on what you need to do on any given day. Your Guardian Angel constantly prays for you and asks God to help you.

Do not worship angels. Worship God only. Guardian Angels are the closest angels to us, and know what we are thinking and feeling. It is important for you to give them permission to speak to you and work with you. A Guardian Angel is not able to bring you the guidance that you need and really talk to you unless you give him or her permission. All you have to do is ask questions of your Guardian Angel and give thanks for the answers he or she gives you. It is important for you to acknowledge his or her presence.

Questions for Your Guardian Angel

* What is your name?
* What can I do to get along with my children better?
* How can I communicate with my children so they understand me better?
* What should I do to improve my financial situation?When will it be the right timing for me to take a trip and travel?
* Is this relationship going to be long-term and lead to marriage?
* Should I go back to school?
* What can I do to have my health restored?
* Should I buy a house or rent?
* Should I look for another job or stay?

Inviting Your Guardian Angel to Contact You: An Exercise

To contact your Guardian Angel, put yourself in a relaxed, quiet state of mind. Then call on your Guardian Angel to come; give the angel permission to speak to you. Begin asking questions. As you quiet your mind, listen for the answers. Most likely, your angel will speak directly into your mind with divine guidance and answers to your questions. It may take some time and practice before you actually "hear" anything from your Guardian Angel. As you relax and get quiet, you will be able to recognize guidance and receive it. It is best to ask specific questions. The more specific you can be with a question, the more specific the answer will be. The Guardian Angel will always help you make the right decision. The angel will present different positive options to you, so you are able to make the right decision for yourself. Our Guardian Angels want us to use our free will.

When I need guidance, I ask my Guardian Angel to speak directly into my mind so I can receive it. Then I wait in silence, in a meditative state, and listen for his response. During the day, a Guardian Angel will often "talk" to you by giving you guidance in a format we would usually think of as intuition or a gut feeling. If you do not hear anything during meditation, do not get discouraged. Your angel will speak to you during the day as you go about your duties. Many times, the Guardian Angel will show you a sign, like a feather or a coin you find on the ground. Sometimes numbers that have meaning for you appear in threes. All these signs show you that your Guardian Angel is nearby and is connecting with you. When he speaks directly into your mind, you may believe that you are just generating your own thoughts or ideas. As you become more familiar with this process, you will recognize the subtle differences between self-generated thoughts and the Guardian Angel's guidance. For example, the sentence structure of an idea may be different, or he will use words that you normally would not. That is how you know it is not you.

Your Guardian Angel can also speak to you in your dreams, during meditation, or when you are driving. If a Guardian Angel wants to get your attention, he may move an object or show you the same number repeatedly in different contexts. Sometimes a Guardian Angel will manifest near you, and you will be able to see him. He may appear to you as an orb of light or a flash of sparkling blue or white light. You will feel very peaceful and will feel a presence of love when you see the light. He may appear to you in a spiritual form. Do not be frightened— embrace the energy. When you know it is your Guardian Angel, you will feel love, peace, and comfort.

Contact Your Guardian Angel: A Guided Meditation

Are you ready to contact your Guardian Angel? Take a quartz crystal and hold it in your left hand. Take a deep breath. Blow it out your nose very quickly. Close your eyes. Visualize your energy moving into the crystal and merging with it. Now visualize the crystal growing as big as a house. Visualize yourself walking down a path. As you walk, you see beautiful flowers, trees, and birds singing all around you. You arrive at the big crystal house and walk up to the door. It is a beautiful door of gold and silver. Open the door. As you walk through the door, on your right-hand side, you see a beautiful fountain and a rainbow above it.

How does it feel inside this house? How is the temperature? Is it warm and comfortable? Is it cold? Look around; what do you see? As you look ahead, you see a stairway. You decide to climb the stairway. It curves around at the top. As you walk, you approach a room on the right. The door is partly open; push open the door completely. As you do, you see a spiritual being made of light. It is a warm, friendly, and comfortable presence—and it is waiting for you. It is your Guardian Angel. Ask the angel's name. The Guardian Angel has something to show you. He or she motions for you to sit down and begins to open a scroll on the table. As you look around you, you see a warm fireplace burning with fire. The room is very comfortable, with lush carpet and beautiful colors all around. You feel very calm and relaxed in the presence of your Guardian Angel. You feel love and the presence of a spiritual light all around you. Walk over to the chair and sit down. Watch as the Guardian Angel manifests in a more physical way. You are able to see him or her very clearly now. Look at the scroll—it contains a special message for you. The angel begins to read you the message, which speaks of your greater purpose and what you are to do in this life. It is all in the scroll, and the scroll is your contract for this life. After hearing, you feel eager to ask questions of the Guardian Angel.

As you sit with the Guardian Angel, ask as many questions as you like. Listen for the answers. After you are satisfied, say good-bye and thank your Guardian Angel. The angel tells you that he or she will be near you at all times; you should make contact if you need anything at all. A Guardian Angel stays with you your whole life and will always give you emotional support and love. You both say good-bye.

Turn, leave the room, and walk back down the stairs. Think about the conversation you had with your Guardian Angel. Leave the house and walk back down the path back to this reality. Visualize the crystal getting smaller and smaller as you do. Then take a deep breath in through your nose and let it out quickly. Release your energy from the crystal, and come back into the present moment. Open your eyes and come back into the room.

You have just experienced a meditation that can help you contact your Guardian Angel. Repeat this meditation to talk to your Guardian Angel anytime. Keep adding rooms to the house—one for each type of direction you are seeking. Envision a conference room if you want to meet different aspects of yourself and consider what type of decision each would make about a given situation. Envision these different aspects of your personality discussing the options in a meeting, just like at the office. Envision a healing or meditation room filled with colored lights if you want to focus on healing your physical body, your emotional body, or your aura. Envision an art studio to help you with creativity. Use your imagination to create whatever environment you feel you need.

Make a list or write in your journal what you experienced during this meditation.

1. _____
2. _____
3. _____
4. _____
5. _____

Recognizing Signs from a Guardian Angel

You may be wondering what types of signs a Guardian Angel might show you. They vary for everyone, but I will share some of the signs that my Guardian Angel has brought to me.

Once, when I was holding a class on past-life regression, a couple of people in the class said that they saw a feather near my head, in the spiritual dimension. I have learned to recognize this sign when my Guardian Angel is letting me know that he is guiding me. In that instance, he was letting me know I was giving the right information to the class. If I see a feather on the ground, I will pick it up—I know my Guardian Angel is near. He is letting me know that everything is going to be okay.

Quarters are often also symbolic for me. At one point, I noticed that I had started seeing quarters on the ground on a regular basis. I picked them up, amused. Then I also started dreaming about quarters. Soon afterward, I noticed that everywhere I went, it seemed like people were dropping quarters accidentally. It got to the point where people were regularly dropping large numbers of quarters when I happened to be around. For example, I was standing near a woman taking the drawer out of a cash register when the drawer started to slip out of her hands—the quarters were the only change that dropped onto the ground. Another time I walked by the pharmacy in an Albertsons, and the same thing happened again. As a sales clerk started taking the drawer out of the cash register, all the quarters came out. I realized in hindsight that my Guardian Angel was trying to show me that a big change was coming into my life. After about six months, my father died, I got a new job, and I moved to another apartment. When your Guardian Angel wants to get your attention or give you a message, the same thing will happen again until you recognize it as a recurring pattern. This quarter situation went on for months.

During the last year, I started seeing the number 222 everywhere. I thought it was odd because two happens to be my least favorite number. It took me about eight months to figure out what it meant. I was about to meet partners in business. That is exactly what has happened. It meant connecting up with others to accomplish my goals and my purpose in this life.

My Guardian Angel will often use symbols or numbers like these to get my attention. It takes me a long time to figure out what he is trying to say to me. Once I recognize that I have been seeing a meaningful pattern, I ask him to speak into my mind whatever it is he wants me to know. In that way, I will know what the guidance or message is right away. I will not have to keep trying to figure it out for weeks or even months. My Guardian Angel usually chooses to speak directly into my mind in the mornings when I wake up—yours may choose another time.

When you receive messages or signs, whether through symbols or through your intuition, you should trust that it is most likely the correct advice. Sometimes we need to evaluate what we have seen or heard and think about it before using it to make a decision. We have to be sure the guidance is coming from God and the angels. We do have free will, so our Guardian Angels can only guide us—we must decide on our actions for ourselves. If you are seeking God, you can feel confident that symbols and signs are guiding you down the path to spiritual growth.

Other spirits may try to give you guidance. How do you discern whether it is correct? Ask the spirit if it comes in the name of Jesus Christ, the Son of God, who died and rose on the third day, overcoming death and the Devil.

If the response is yes, then you know it is worthy guidance coming through. It is not good enough for an entity just to acknowledge Jesus Christ—it must believe he is the Son of God. This is how you can tell the difference between correct guidance and false guidance. Spirits can disguise themselves as angels of light. Before you contact your angels, always protect yourself with the protection and grounding techniques we learned in Chapter 2.

You can also tell if it is true guidance by whether you feel love and peace. You will know by the presence and the higher vibrational frequency of love and light. Any guidance that feels demanding, scary, or aggressive is not from the angels. Think back to a time when you felt you received guidance in some way, but you were not sure what to do about it. Normally, if you have doubts about the decision you are making, it is best to delay making that decision until you feel more certain.

Sometimes guidance is very clear. Have you ever woke up in the morning, because you thought you heard someone calling your name? That happened to me one morning—but there was no one around except my cat. I knew, therefore, that it must be my Guardian Angel.

Another time, I went into the bathroom at work and heard a loud horn blowing. The sound was so loud in my ear that it really startled me—then I realized the bathroom was otherwise quiet. The noise was not coming from any outside source. It made me remember that I had a dream the night before about a Mayan bell ringing. The horn lasted for about five minutes, and it really began to hurt my ear. I could not believe it was happening—I knew immediately it was a sign and related to the Mayan bell ringing in my dream. The dream had been about new beginnings in my life. Then I realized the horn blowing in my ear was making me think about Archangel Gabriel, who is associated with blowing a horn to announce something new. After that, new beginnings did indeed take place in my life. I bought and moved to a new home. Then there was a lay-off at my job. Then I got another job. It is important to become aware of the signs that the angels and spirit guides bring us to enable us to make the right decisions.

How Guardian Angels Use Intuition to Relay Messages

When you feel like you have understood something instantly, intuitively, without having to think about it, it may be because it was your Guardian Angel speaking to you by placing thoughts directly into your mind. In 2008, I was driving to work, and I came to an intersection. I intended to turn left, and the traffic light was green. I looked both ways—clear. It was three o'clock on a Friday afternoon. Suddenly, I just felt very strange. Something was not right. My gut and intuition said something was wrong, but I could not figure out what it was—the situation was normal enough. I felt very happy in general, and I had been listening to a Christian radio station and was thanking God and praising God as I drove. The nagging feeling that something suddenly was not right was overwhelming. I looked around the intersection, but I did not see one other car. I felt like I was in another dimension or time zone. It was eerie, to be honest. At that time, the intersection should have been very busy, with a lot of traffic. I knew, because I drove that same way every day. I had a green light, though, so I proceeded into the intersection. I did not listen to my intuition.

All of a sudden, I felt something hit my van. I heard a big bang and the van started spinning. I instantly realized I had been in an accident. I only had time to wonder how it could have happened, since the road had been clear, before I lost consciousness. A truck had indeed run a red light and hit me on the driver's side. He hit me hard enough to total my van. Somehow, I came away with only bruises on my left side and some whiplash in my neck. Other than that, I was fine. I was not bleeding; I did not break any bones. I know my Guardian Angel protected me.

This is an example of not listening to your intuition or gut feeling. It was a hard way for me to learn to pay attention to my intuition. If you have any doubts at all or feel something is not right, it is important to stop what you are doing until you figure out why. Even though I had a green light and nobody was around, I knew there was something wrong. I did not stop. I made a terrible mistake. From that experience, I have learned to listen to my gut feelings and my intuition. I do now!

What is strange about the whole story, though, is that I had been listening to a CD just a few minutes earlier that was discussing how sometimes you have to get in an accident to grow spiritually or to become enlightened. I had just turned off the CD and turned on the Christian radio station about five minutes before the accident. I was very happy and felt good. I was in a higher consciousness state. As I look back now, I believe that my subconscious mind took in the statement about getting in an accident and somehow put me in a situation where I would. Yes, I grew spiritually because of it. After that accident, I decided to listen only to music CDs in the car! It also showed me how powerful the subconscious mind is and how we create our own reality by our thinking. This was a powerful lesson for me. If I am in a relaxed state, as I was while driving that day, my subconscious mind can pick up ideas I hear and then act on them. Your Guardian Angel will try to warn you through your intuition and gut feelings. Remember to pay attention and listen—for your own safety.

Think about your own life. Were there times when you listened to your intuition? Can you list the times when you did not listen to your intuition?

1. _____
2. _____
3. _____
4. _____

Looking Back

Have you ever been warned and realize you did not listen and something unfortunate happened? We all have. We must recognize when our Guardian Angels are trying to communicate with us. It can save us a lot of heartache and trouble.

I used to live in Sedona, Arizona. I had planned a trip to Flagstaff, and the day before I was due to leave, three different people told me not to go. These three people did not know one another. I was stubborn and did not listen, because I was excited. The next day, I got in my car and started to drive to Flagstaff. About fifteen minutes into the drive, I was going up a curvy road. A car came out of nowhere, in front of me. I was going about forty-five miles an hour at the time. There was no intersection or cross street. Suddenly a car was there, turning in the same direction, I was going, and it was only five or eight inches away. I could see the driver—she was an older woman and was only going about five miles an hour. I recognized immediately that it was going to be humanly impossible for that car not to hit my car. The thought went through my mind, "I'm going to be in an accident."

Suddenly I heard a voice telling me to turn the steering wheel to the left. After that, I do not remember anything. I lost consciousness. I do not actually remember turning the wheel to the left. When I woke up, I found myself on the other side of the road, facing the opposite direction. My car had stopped and the engine was off. I know that the angels somehow moved my car over to the other side of the road. I looked up, thankful to be alive. I praised God and saw that all the other cars coming down the road had stopped. The drivers' mouths were open in disbelief. It was as if they had seen a miracle. It all happened so fast. The car that had pulled out in front of me was nowhere to be seen.

Now, you would think that would be enough to make me turn around and go back to Sedona. Back in 1995, I was stubborn. I continued up the road to Flagstaff. I was almost there when it started raining hard. I came to a section of road where there was a solid wall of water in front of me. I had never seen anything like it. It was about seven feet tall, and it crossed the whole road. I was adventurous and determined to go through it. When I started to go through, I could not see anything at all. I continued driving but eventually had to pull over because I could not see anything. Eventually, the storm eased up.

My destination was a religious store in Flagstaff. I knew the owner, and I was planning a visit to him. I finally arrived. It was still raining. There was construction going on, so between that and the rain, I had a hard time trying to find a place to park. When I finally found a spot, I got out, walked through the water, and went into the store. I said hello to the owner, and he asked if I needed any help. I told him I had felt pulled to come up to his store for a reason, but I was not sure what it was. I said, "I am not going to leave this store until I get the message." Then he asked whether I was planning to attend a Buddhist dance ceremony that was going to take place back in Sedona. I looked at him and said, "That's it!" I had forgotten all about the Buddhist ceremony.

I turned around and looked outside the store. There was not one drop of water anywhere. Neither of us saw any water. We could not believe our eyes. It seemed impossible. I had just fought through all that water and flooding to get to the store, and I had only been there for ten or fifteen minutes. To this day, we cannot figure out what happened. When I left a little while later, there was no sign of any rainwater anywhere. The rest of my day went beautifully. Not one other negative thing happened after that. All the bad luck was gone.

I drove back down to Sedona and went to the Buddhist dance ceremony. When I left the celebration, I realized that I had been healed of a stomach problem

I was having. If I had not gone to Flagstaff, I would not have heard about the Buddhist ceremony and would not have been healed by the ceremony. I still wonder about that day. People told me not to go up to Flagstaff because there was danger, and I could have been in an accident. My Guardian Angel saved me and rescued me from a terrible fate. So on one hand, if I had not been stubborn and gone up to Flagstaff, I would not have received healing because my friend would not have reminded me about the Buddhist ceremony. On the other hand, when I took a risk and went up there, the angels turned bad luck to good and gave me a message. They turned lemons into lemonade.

In my life, there have been times when I have been very foolish and put my life at risk. Now that I am older, I do not put my life at risk anymore if I can help it. It is best to listen to your intuition or to people that may give you a warning about something. You never know—it could be your angels talking to you through other people, which they do. I believe that my Guardian Angel spoke to me to turn the wheel to the left and moved the car over to the other side of the road. He protected me.

A Guardian Angel's Point of View on Working with Us

Have you ever wondered what your Guardian Angel thinks about you? How does a Guardian Angel see you?

Guardian Angels have never been born in a human body. They are supernatural spiritual beings full of love toward us. They only want the best for us. They may think that we are unwilling to listen at times, but they have our best interests at heart and will continue to watch over us and encourage us. Their job is to comfort us and protect us. They are all love and light. They have chosen this job to work with us. They will never give up on us.

Your Guardian Angels have this message for you: "We have been here since you were born. We will help you fulfill your purpose in life. We will guide you and watch over you throughout your whole life. As your Guardian Angels, we will help you learn the lessons you chose to learn before you came to Earth in a human body. We see God's plan and can assist you with our different areas of expertise. We often appear to you as colored, sparkling lights. Ask us for what you want, and watch for signs that you have been heard. You may ask us any question at all. If you put your intention to have us be in your dreams, we will come. Some of you have blocks in your minds, and because of your upbringing or conditioning, you feel you cannot fulfill your purpose. We will try to help you overcome these blocks and conflicts. We will show you the direction you need to go. We enjoy working with each one of you. We come from a place of love and compassion. We will shower you with peace and an assurance that you will be always loved."

"We will bring you signs and synchronicities to get your attention and to show you things that you need to know to guide you on your path. When we need to intervene in your life, we do this in various ways. We give you good ideas and flashes of insight. We speak through your intuition as thoughts that come out of nowhere. This is how we send you important information. We arrange for you to meet certain people for a particular reason. We send people into your life to help you and point you in a certain direction for you to fulfill your purpose. Delays in what you want to do might come for a reason. Timing is everything. We will have you at the right place at the right time to connect with the right people. This will be according to God's will for your life and what you have chosen to do. We can also speak through people you know to give you messages. We might also send you strangers to give you messages. You can hear, see, and feel us. Just pay attention to our guidance in meditation. Listen to your intuition and follow it. If something does not feel right, it probably is not. Sometimes we will place a high-pitched ringing noise in your ear. We are sending you messages and downloading information into your being, which you may access later. Remember to call on us and give us permission to help you. We will always be with you."

—*Channeled from my Guardian Angel*

Can you look back on your life and remember when you saw signs that you now recognize as being from your Guardian Angel, or when you noticed synchronicities in your life? List them or write them down in a journal.

1. _____

2. _____

3. _____

4. _____

5. _____

Summary of Key Points

- You must call on your Guardian Angel and give him or her permission to help you.
- To contact your angel, go into a meditative state by quieting your mind and relaxing. Ask specific questions of your Guardian Angel in meditation.
- Know that your Guardian Angel's responses may come to you as ideas and thoughts that come spontaneously into your mind.
- Learn to recognize recurring themes, situations, or objects in your life as signs and synchronicities from your Guardian Angel.
- Listen to your intuition and your gut feelings, and follow them—they may be your Guardian Angel telling you something.

CHAPTER 4

RECEIVING MORE GUIDANCE FROM THE ANGELS, SPIRIT GUIDES, AND DECEASED LOVED ONES

———

Trust in the Lord with all thine heart; and
lean not unto thine own understanding.
In all thy ways acknowledge him,
and he shall direct thy paths.

—*Proverbs 3:5–6 KJV*

In the last chapter, we learned about Guardian Angels. We learned how you can contact and hear from your Guardian Angel. We went through a meditative exercise and learned how important it is to listen to your intuition and gut feelings, and to follow them. In this chapter, we will continue to talk about how our Guardian Angels communicate with us. Other spirits, such as deceased loved ones and spirit guides, will want to communicate with us also. True guidance, and false guidance, and how to discern the difference will be explained. We will also talk about dreams and journal writing.

How Angels Communicate with Us

You may wonder whether the angels are aware of our thoughts and prayers. Angels do hear our prayers and respond to them. God knows everything we think. Send prayers to God while calling on the angels. The most important thing to remember is to put God first, and to worship God only. Guardian Angels and all the other angels are messengers that come from God.

As we learned in the last chapter, your Guardian Angel can communicate with you in several ways. He or she may place thoughts directly into your mind. Other times, you will see pictures in your mind, or simply feel love or peace. Most of the time, however, the angels will give you signs to try to get your attention. After I asked my Guardian Angel to speak into my mind directly, I would receive flashes of insight about what to do. Sometimes I would also see clear pictures in my mind. This was so much easier for me than trying to figure out the meaning behind a sign or synchronicity that the angel was sending to me. Flashes of insight can come at any time, during or after your meditation or quiet time. Your Guardian Angel can also set up circumstances for an event to happen to you. The angel does this to get you to look toward another direction with your life or to get your attention.

Here is an example from my own life. The angels wanted me to cut back to working three days a week instead of five.

I just could not do it. Survival issues came up, and my ego balked at the idea. I wanted to follow the angels, but something inside me said no. I was afraid to make such a big change, so I tried not to listen even though the message was very clear. I knew if I did not choose to start working part-time, something would happen to make me cut my hours. I ignored the warning. A month later, a health issue forced me to go down to three days a week. Please listen to your angels! I now know that the angels wanted me to cut to three days a week so I would have time to work on this book. Since then, I wake up in the morning and ask my angels, "What do you want me to do this day, before I go to work?" I always get an answer from them. They direct me to do what I need to do for that day to fulfill my larger purpose in life. My angels always tell me the next step I need to take to accomplish my goal.

The angels will always show you signs to acknowledge that they have heard your requests and are watching over you. You should also trust that your Guardian Angel will protect you during a crisis. The angels are always sending you messages, you just need to train yourself to listen. Signs from the angels guide us and tell us we are going in the right direction and doing what we are supposed to be doing.

True Guidance Versus False Guidance

*For Satan Himself is transformed
into an angel of light.*

—*2 Corinthians 11:14 KJV*

Regard not them that have familiar spirits,
neither seek after wizards, to be defiled
by them: I am the Lord your God.

—*LEVITICUS 19:31 KJV*

How do you discern the difference between true guidance and false guidance? You will know through your intuition and feel surrounded by love. You may see different-colored lights in meditation or receive flashes of insight and new ideas.

Here is a personal example of guidance by my Guardian Angel. I asked him where I put a favorite ring that I could not find. Then I saw a picture within my mind of the place in my home where it was. He could not have told me where it was any more clearly. I went there, and sure enough, I found the ring. When you follow the guidance of the angels, you will feel at peace and know that you are on the right track and making the right decisions.

When you are not following their guidance, you will become frustrated and stuck. False guidance makes you feel pressured to make a decision that you are not sure about, or to make a decision out of a concern for survival. You will impulsively make a decision without thinking about it. False guidance can come from your ego or a lower vibrational entity.

Whereas your rational mind will drive you toward finding knowledge, your ego will just try to keep you feeling safe. You experience fear and anxiety when the ego tries to stop you from taking a risk and following your intuition. Listening to your intuition sometimes does not seem to make rational sense. As you take a risk, however, you will find that it will bring you to your life's purpose. There are many voices that we listen to every day, both from the spiritual realms and within our own mind. These different voices come from spirit guides, our ego, our rational mind, negative spirits, entities, angels, and the Holy Spirit.

True guidance will bring you peace, love, and a nurturing feeling. It will come in the form of gentle, repeated messages. It will bring you different options and choices. False guidance will make you feel controlled. It will be very demanding, and will bring fear and anxiety to you. This guidance will feel selfish and will not benefit other people. You will feel confused by your options and feel like you are not able to think straight. You will feel an urgency about making a decision and feel guilty when you do not. The options will feel forced upon you. This guidance is usually negative in nature, and given by a spirit guide or stems from a negative spirit in your life. The ego and the rational mind will also remind you of survival issues, such as immediate cash flow, and make you feel that you must act immediately, whether or not you feel good about the decision.

When we work with the Holy Spirit to receive guidance, we know with certainly that we will be getting positive, helpful guidance. The Holy Spirit will lead you into all truth because he is of God. The Holy Spirit is wisdom. As we work with the Holy Spirit, we will make clear decisions that will help us move towards the will of God and purpose for our life. He speaks to us by a still, small voice within. As we praise and worship God, the presence of God comes down as the Holy Spirit. Ask the Holy Spirit daily to go before you and prepare the way so you will be protected and have a peaceful, happy day. As we abide in Christ and his word, we will receive guidance and protection.

Many spirit guides are deceased relatives or people we knew in past lives. Most have good intentions and want to guide you and help you. Different spirit guides have different levels of expertise and spiritual authority. Not all spirit guides have developed a higher consciousness, nor are they spiritually "mature."

I worked with the Archangels directly for a while, but then I began thinking about my Guardian Angel. I decided to call on my Guardian Angel and give him permission to bring me guidance. Once I acknowledged him, I realized he had rescued me during those car accidents. He had been with me all along, through many difficult times. In a sense, I was contacting Archangels before I started contacting my own Guardian Angel. Usually, people do it the other way around!

We must learn to discern the different types of guidance that come through. You do have free will and have the choice to listen to the guidance or not, depending on how you feel about it. If it is positive guidance that empowers you with love and self-confidence, you know it is true guidance. You will feel comfort and a nurturing feeling with true guidance. Never follow guidance out of desperation. True guidance will be soft and gentle and will encourage you to make changes in your life that deep down you already know you need to make. Angels will bring guidance to you through visions, dreams, signs, or they will speak directly into your mind or show you mental images.

We can make decisions either out of fear or love. We already know which is preferable and helpful.

Guidance Through Dreams

Have you ever wondered what messages your dreams are trying to send you?

Guidance that comes to you in your dreams from God and the angels will be loving and positive. Your job is to interpret how that guidance can fit into your life. You can ask your Guardian Angel, "What is the meaning of this dream?" You may have thought it meant one thing when the dream really means something else. It is best to call on Jesus Christ and the Holy Spirit to clarify the messages in your dreams. Any guidance that seems to threaten you, or is demanding and controlling, is false guidance. You have the choice to accept it or not. You do have choices in life. By tuning in to your intuition, you will be able to tell the difference between true guidance and false guidance. If you place protection around yourself before you go to sleep and ask your Guardian Angel to speak to you in your dreams, you will probably get true guidance.

You should evaluate every piece of guidance that seems to be coming through your dreams. Sometimes, other spirits may be trying to give you guidance. You must discern whether it is of God or not of God. To do this, you can ask the spirit or the guide if it believes that Jesus Christ, the Son of God, came in the flesh, died, rose again on the third day, and overcame death. If the spirit says that it does, then it is probably true guidance. Always ask yourself what type of guidance it seems to be as well—any guidance that creates fear, criticism, or punishment is false guidance.

Do not just open yourself up to any spiritual being that wants to communicate with you. This can be very dangerous. Always call on Archangel Michael to come and protect you before you meditate for guidance. Always visualize and place a white light around you while you meditate as well.

Getting back to dreams—if you cannot remember a whole dream, that is okay. Write down or record whatever you can remember either in a journal, on a tape recorder, or with your cell phone's recorder. When you first wake up, the dream should be fresh in your mind. Immediately write it down before it dissipates. If you are having a hard time remembering your dreams, ask your angels to help you remember. Angels will come in your dreams and bring you messages in your dream state. As you practice and do this every morning, you will get better at remembering your dreams. If you use a voice recorder and speak out what was in your dream, you can listen to it later. Using a voice recorder may be easier than writing something down if you are half-asleep. Voice recordings often capture more details from a dream because you can say them quickly, without having to take the time to write.

Angels can Communicate with Us in our Dreams

Angels can and do give us guidance through our dreams. For example, I had a dream where I was driving my car in a certain direction. I saw a roadblock that made me turn around. Before I turned around, however, I felt an urge to make a side trip over to a building to run an errand. Something in the dream told me it would be important to just turn around and go the other direction and not to stop. When I woke up, I realized what the dream was telling me. I was becoming distracted by small projects in my life. I needed to look at my priorities and go after my main goal, and to focus intently on accomplishing it. It was also telling me to reevaluate my goals and be sure that I was going the right direction in life to fulfill my purpose. I had to look at my path in life, because it was possible I was going the wrong direction. I needed to stop and consider what it might mean to turn around and go back the way I came.

Angels Notify Us of Changes to Come

Angels do not always just provide guidance to us; sometimes they make outright announcements about things that are inevitable. I had a recurring dream warning me about big changes that would soon come into my life. I kept dreaming about the ocean, large waves, and flooding. These dreams went on for about a year. Then, physical flooding started occurring in my life. One day, the water would not turn off in my home, and I had to turn it off manually outside. Then an actual flood occurred in my area— destroying many homes, but mine was not affected. When I went to work another day, I found the store had flooded—three inches of water covered the floor, but I had to sweep out the water and open for business. Then another time, I was at the laundromat and my clothes were in the washing machine when the electricity went out. I had to take all the clothes out of the water. Everywhere there was some kind of water situation! My father also fell ill and died during that time. I ended up moving and changing jobs. I realized that, for me, water represents big changes in my life.

I encourage you to keep a dream journal and to write down your dreams every morning so you can find similar meaningful patterns.

Summary of Key Points

* Trust and follow your intuition.
* Pay attention to how you feel about the situation.
* Listen for guidance in meditation.
* Pay attention to your gut feelings.
* Accept the visions that come to you from the higher levels of consciousness.
* Make choices depending on whether you feel peaceful or not.
* Before going to sleep each night, ask a question of your Guardian Angel.

CHAPTER 5

WORKING WITH THE ARCHANGELS AND DISCOVERING THEIR SPECIALTIES

———

Who is gone into heaven, and is on the right hand of God; angels and authorities and powers being made subject unto him.

—*I Peter 3:22 KJV*

Have you ever wondered what each Archangel does, or how to make contact with a specific Archangel?

In the last chapter, we talked about receiving messages from Guardian Angels and how to recognize true guidance versus false guidance. We also talked about how your Guardian Angel can give you guidance through your dreams and your intuition. In this chapter, I will introduce you to what each Archangel does and his specialty in providing you with information about God's direction for your life. I will also tell you about each Ascended Master who is associated with each Archangel.

Who are the Archangels?

You may wonder: Who are the Archangels and what do they do?

Archangels are divine spiritual beings of the highest vibration that God created to do God's work according to His will. They bring messages from God to humanity. They are very powerful and loving beings, and their job is to carry out the will of God. Each one represents an aspect of God. Archangels can be many places at one time and can help people in different locations at the same time. Archangels have very high levels of consciousness and vibration. Archangels have many angels working under them. The Archangels are in charge of Guardian Angels, and they give the Guardian Angels messages for us as guidance. The Archangels will do whatever is necessary to help everybody fulfill his or her purpose according to God's will.

Each Archangel has a specialty that covers a different department of life. All are happy to assist you. All you have to do is call on a particular Archangel and give him permission to help you with a particular problem. I have experienced a lot of miracles and supernatural events by calling on the Archangels for help directly. Each Archangel has a specialty, a color flame, a gemstone, and an Ascended Master associated with him. If you work with gemstones, you can connect with the Archangels through a gemstone meditation exercise. These meditations will be covered under each Archangel mentioned within this chapter.

Archangels are messengers of God and are not to be worshipped. We simply call on angels and give them permission to help us. Call on the Archangels to assist you in finding your path according to God's will and to help you in everyday life. Your focus should be putting God first. He is the creator, the Almighty God, and our goal should be to accept His plan for our lives. Archangels will not interfere with your free will. If you do not give them permission, they cannot help you—unless it is a crisis or emergency. In a life-threatening situation, the angels can automatically come and help you. As you develop a relationship with any of the Archangels, you will be able to have conversations and talk with them at any time.

It is good to learn about the Archangels' specialties so you can call on them when you encounter a situation that requires a specific type of help. For example, Archangel Michael protects against negativity. Therefore, he is a good one to have on your side when you need protection against the negative forces that may come against you.

If you want to work with the Archangels and bring them around you, focus on your spiritual life and self-development. As you become more pure in your thinking, more positive and optimistic, the angels will flock around you. The closer you get to God through worship and praise, the closer the Archangels will come to you. It all comes down to your intentions and motives for the things that you do. We must be aware of our thinking patterns to be able to change them. Focusing our thoughts and expressing positive words is a process of spiritual growth. We learn lessons as we go through life.

The Archangels worship and serve God. I usually get messages from the Archangels first thing in the morning. When I meditate, I quiet my mind and open myself up to receive guidance. I usually follow their instructions, because I have found that when I do, everything just goes more smoothly. I have learned to trust them. I always ask the Archangels to go before me and prepare the way for a peaceful, prosperous, and harmonious day. I ask them to connect me with the right people at the right time to fulfill my purpose. I have learned to identify many synchronicities in my life as they happen.

The Archangels' purpose is to do whatever is needed to help every person be at peace and accomplish his or her purpose on Earth. The Archangels are helpers, guides, and protectors. God instructs the Archangels and sends them to help us when we have called on them and given them permission.

Always pray to God before you call on the Archangels. When you call on Archangels and give them permission to help you, do it aloud. Saying it aloud is more powerful because you are adding sound to your intention. For example, if you need protection, call on Archangel Michael to come and protect you from a particular person you are with. You can say it in your mind and, if you have already given permission for the Archangel to help you, he will be able to hear you. It will still be effective. After you explain the situation or problem, then release it to the Archangel. Let him take it from you. Thank the Archangel for his help and service, and give praise to God again. Be sure to follow any guidance that the Archangels give you, which may manifest as ideas that come into your mind. The Archangels often speak to us through our intuition.

When an Archangel is near you, you may feel a tingling sensation, a loving presence, or see colored, sparkling lights. You may find that you suddenly know something, and cannot logically explain how you came to know it. You might know that something is about to happen. You may receive messages or flashes of insight through your intuition. If you ask an Archangel for a sign, you can receive one by starting to see how everything is in harmony and fits together. Be sure to thank the Archangels and God for guiding you.

Ascended Masters are spiritually enlightened beings that have gained great knowledge about the physical plane as well as the spiritual realms, and so have attained the initiations needed for enlightenment and the ascension. They have attained oneness with the divine. They have recognized that God's spirit is within them and have discovered that meditation is the key to accessing God and attaining oneness with Him. They have overcome obstacles on the spiritual path, and have learned all the lessons that were set out for them to learn. Now they assist and serve others in their spiritual growth. If we acknowledge the different Ascended Masters, they will assist us in our own ascension process. They will encourage us to learn our lessons in this life. We must decide to learn these lessons for our spiritual growth. On the other side, we decided with our spiritual master teachers and guides what lessons we would need to learn during our current lifetimes for our spiritual development. The Ascended Masters work with us when we are sleeping and take us to their retreats for learning and soul development. Before you go to sleep and dream, ask an Ascended Master to take you to his or her retreat for learning. Each Ascended Master has an association with an Archangel. They work together according to their specialties, as teams that serve humanity. As we acknowledge that we do have a spiritual family of ascended beings and angels, we can be assured that we are never alone and will always be guided in the right direction according to God's divine will.

The Archangels' Specialties and Related Ascended Masters

This is a list of the Archangels' specialties and how they help us in specific situations. It includes each Ascended Master who works with them.

Archangel Ariel

Archangel Ariel has been mentioned in the books of Judaic mysticism. He works with the fairies and nature spirits and directs their activities. He is associated with the Ascended Master Kuthumi. In a past incarnation, Kuthumi was Pythagoras, who worked with sacred geometry and musical tones for healing. He was also Francis of Assisi in a past life who could communicate with animals. He established a mystery school. If you want knowledge, call on him and ask him to work with you. Archangel Ariel is also associated with the Ascended Master Djwal Khul. He was called the Tibetan and was taught under the Ascended Master

Kuthumi. He brings wisdom, love, and compassion. He transmitted his teachings through Alice Bailey from 1919 to 1949. He was last seen in the 1800s before his ascension.

Specialties of Archangel Ariel include:

* Healing animals
* Healing of the environment
* Bringing you courage and self-confidence
* Helping you to manifest prosperity and abundance
* Bringing you new opportunities
* Bringing you good luck

Color Flames: olive green and pink

Olive green is the color of prosperity and abundance. Visualize olive green around you. Pink is the color of unconditional love. It is an antiaging color and brings youthfulness. Throughout the day, breathe in the pink color, having it circulate throughout your body. Visualize the color pink as you breathe it in.

Gemstones: rose quartz, pink sapphire, and peridot

Gemstone Meditation

Place a rose quartz gemstone in your left hand, or visualize one there. Now close your eyes, breathe in through your nose, and out quickly, becoming one with the rose quartz. Now you are inside the rose quartz on an energy level. Look around inside this crystal, and what do you see? How does it feel? All of a sudden, Archangel Ariel is there with you and is asking you to follow him into the manifestation room, where prosperity and abundance can be yours. As you follow him into the manifestation room, you get excited with anticipation of what is going to happen. You start thinking about your dreams and what you want to manifest. As you approach the door of this room, it begins to open for you.

Archangel Ariel walks with you into the room and asks you to lie down on this bed. He explains that your body will be infused by a color of prosperity. Then you see an olive-green light with gold specks floating down, absorbing into your body. Archangel Ariel asks you to visualize that your dreams have already come true. You follow his instructions. You believe, and feel this prosperous energy fill your body. Now you know with confidence that your dreams are in the process of happening. Archangel Ariel tells you the process has been completed and it is time to leave the manifestation room. As you leave and walk through this rose quartz crystal, you feel this divine love and prosperity come over you. Now you are ready to receive the prosperity that is yours in this life. Archangel Ariel tells you, "I will be around you and will help you; just call on me." You thank him and then find yourself in the rose-quartz crystal, ready to return. As you breathe in and out quickly through your nose, releasing yourself from the rose quartz, you open your eyes and come back into the room.

Archangel Ariel's Suggested Exercise

Take time out to go into nature and walk among the trees, feeling the soil within your hands and under your feet. As you are walking, take deep breaths and take your time to enjoy the nature all around you. Look for little animals and birds. Listen to the sounds and see the details of nature expressing itself. Relax and realize there is nothing else to do but enjoy the sounds of nature and the peace all around you.

Questions for Archangel Ariel

* Can you connect me with the right people at the right time for new opportunities?
* I ask that you show me ways to experience abundance in my life.
* Can you bring opportunities so I can achieve prosperity in my life or added income?
* Can you heal and restore my pet's health?
* I ask that you encourage me and guide me to the right inspiration so I can have a positive mindset for prosperity.
* I ask you to calm down my pet who is over anxious.

Message from Archangel Ariel

I will help you protect nature and the environment, and I will heal your pets. I will open doors for you so you will meet the right people at the right time to achieve your goals and dreams. I will watch over your pets with love and healing. Good luck will follow you. Focus on what you want. What are your dreams? You can list them here.

1. _____
2. _____
3. _____

A Vision of Archangel Ariel

I had a vision of Archangel Ariel once. It was in the middle of the night—or at around three o'clock in the morning. I had called on him to heal my cat before I went to sleep. I woke up and looked up to see him hovering over my cat Shawnee. The cat had bumped into a table while running and had pulled a muscle in his leg. It had happened about three months earlier, and it had not healed properly. The cat could still not run. I had taken him to the veterinarian, of course, but the vet said there was nothing they could do; it would just have to heal on its own. Shawnee used to run with my other cat through the house, back and forth. It was sad to have to watch the other cat run without him since the accident.

The Archangel was olive green, and at first his wings were moving so fast, I could not see them. Then, all of a sudden, the wings stopped, and he was levitating, stationary, in the air. The wings were very large in proportion to his body, and were olive green in color finely netted. They were shimmery, translucent, and very beautiful. The wings were a round shape; about one foot by one foot in diameter, and the body was probably just about an inch wide and very long. His wings did not make any noise when they flapped. I was shocked and amazed. I could not believe it. I had never seen an angel before that night. After about a minute, he disappeared. I somehow managed to get back to sleep even though I recognized I had seen into another dimension! The Archangel appeared physically, but he was clearly a spiritual being.

When I woke up the next morning, I thought to myself; what did I see last night? Then I remembered I had prayed for the cat to be healed. Soon afterward, Shawnee started running with the other cat again. He had been healed. I thanked Archangel Ariel. Then I put two and two together.

I did some research about Archangels after that, to educate myself about their sizes and colors. It turns out that they manifest themselves in whatever way the person who sees them will expect.

Archangel Azrael

Archangel Azrael is the angel of death. He helps people cross over at the time of physical death. He is found in the Hebrew texts and in the Muslim texts. He is associated with the Ascended Master Kuthumi, who brings healing, love, wisdom, and truth. In a past incarnation, Kuthumi was Pythagoras, who worked with music and sacred geometry in healing. As Francis of Assisi, he could communicate with the animals and nature. He brought peace and healing to his surroundings.

Specialties of Archangel Azrael include:

* Helping people cross over to the other side after death
* Guiding the deceased into the light

- Helping people prepare for death
- Comforting those who are grieving

Color Flame: creamy white-yellow

The color white-yellow represents personal will, personal power, self-control, and removes fear. It is good for stimulating the nervous system and the digestive system.

Gemstone: yellow calcite

Gemstone Meditation

As you hold a yellow calcite in your hands, imagine it getting as big as a house for you to walk into. As your eyes are closed, take a deep breath through your nose, and let it out your nose very quickly, becoming one with the gemstone. As you enter the stone, you will find Archangel Azrael within, asking if you are prepared for death or want comfort if you are grieving over a death. He will assist you in the grieving process. Listen to what he has to say. He has good advice for preparing you for death or if you are grieving over a death of a loved one. Once you receive his messages, you can return by walking out of the yellow calcite and taking a breath quickly in and out through your nose, releasing yourself from the yellow calcite. As you open your eyes, come back to the present time in this reality, and back into the room feeling very peaceful.

Archangel Azrael's Suggested Exercise

If you are by the side of your loved one before death, be sure to send your loved one unconditional love and forgiveness. Ask your loved one who he or she sees in the other dimension before they cross over. Visualize love and light around them as they cross over.

Questions for Archangel Azrael

* Can you assist my loved ones to cross over to the other side?
* Can you send divine comfort and help as I grieve after my loved one's death.
* Can you help guide my loved one into the light?
* Can you help me to prepare for my death so I will be ready?

Message from Archangel Azrael

Call on me to help you with grief. I will help your loved ones cross over to the other side after they die. I will assist you with sending ghosts and your deceased loved ones into the light. I will also assist you in preparing your loved ones for death. Be sure to send your loved ones unconditional love and forgiveness to help them make a peaceful transition into the light.

Archangel Chamuel

You will find Archangel Chamuel in the Kabbalah texts in the Judaic tradition. He is associated with the Ascended Master Maha Chohan, who brought the flame of the Holy Spirit down upon the disciples after Jesus Christ rose from the dead. Maha Chohan now brings the flame of the Holy Spirit to humanity. He is in charge of the powers of nature and the elementals of earth, water, air, and fire. He provides the energy for supernatural manifestations within the physical plane. In his past incarnation, he was a blind man and would recite poetry among the people. He was very creative, and everybody was amazed at his ability. The people called him the poet.

Specialties of Archangel Chamuel include:
* Helping you find employment or lost items
* Directing you into your true life's purpose
* Connecting you with your soulmate

Color Flame: pale green and pink
Pale green is a soothing color and brings peace to the mind while calming the nervous system. It also strengthens the immune system. Use this color to bring about harmony in relationships. The color pink is of the heart and will connect you with love.
Gemstones: peridot, variscite, fluorite, and rose quartz

Gemstone Meditation

Hold a fluorite or stone of your choice in your left hand. Take a breath through your nose, and release it quickly as you become one with the gemstone. Now you find yourself within the gemstone, walking along and seeing beautiful green colors all around. Then you see a stairway leading up into a room. You walk up the stairway and step into the room, and you find yourself within your own heart. As you look around, you see the hurts and the wounds of the heart from the past. You feel compassion and want to heal your own heart. Archangel Chamuel comes on the scene, and tells you to heal your heart through the pink color of unconditional divine love for yourself. He helps you channel God's love to your heart to heal the wounds and the hurts within. As God's energy fills your heart with love, you begin to love and accept yourself for who you truly are; healing begins to happen. As you forgive yourself and others, the wounds and the hurts within the heart begin to heal. The sadness is then replaced with joy. You are so grateful and happy that these colors of green and pink have come upon your heart with God's healing love. Archangel Chamuel stands beside you and assures you that now that your heart is healed, you will attract a loving relationship. You have been waiting for your soulmate and are excited and expectant. You thank Archangel Chamuel for assisting you at this time. He walks with you through the room and back down the stairs, guiding you out through the gemstone to come back into the room alert and awake in the present time. You feel happy, strong, and thankful, as you release yourself from the gemstone by breathing quickly in and out through your nose.

Archangel Chamuel's Suggested Exercise

Call on him to find any lost items. Quiet your mind and listen to Archangel Chamuel as he sends a picture image into your mind where the lost item is. Be sure to give thanks.

Another Exercise Suggested by Archangel Chamuel

If you are seeking employment, and you come across a job you really would like to have, make a decision in your mind that you will have that job. Then imagine your energy cord to the new job. If you're having a hard time leaving your old job, then visualize the cords being cut by Archangel Chamuel that have connected you to the old job. This will release you from the old job and connect you to the new job.

Questions for Archangel Chamuel

* I ask you to assist me in finding a job that will be beneficial for me.
* Can you direct me to my life's purpose and service in this life?
* I ask you to connect me up with my soulmate for my spiritual growth.

Message from Archangel Chamuel

I will help you be at the right place at the right time to connect you to a wonderful and fulfilling relationship. I encourage you to visualize love and harmony in your relationship. Make a list of what you can do now to improve your relationship.

1. _____
2. _____
3. _____

Archangel Gabriel

Archangel Gabriel is found in the book of Daniel 8:15–17, appearing to Daniel in the Christian tradition. He is also found in the book of Enoch. *"Gabriel, one of the holy angels, who presides over Ikisat, over paradise, and over the cherubim"* (Enoch 20:7). He is within the Judaic tradition found in the Mystical Kabbalah. He is associated with the Ascended Master Serapis Bey who is in charge of the white fire flame of purification. Serapis Bey is associated with the Temple of Ascension at Luxor within Egypt. In his past incarnation, he lived as Amenhotep III in Egypt and commissioned the Luxor Temple to be built in Egypt. He continues to train and assist people for moving into the ascension. He ascended around 400 B.C.

Specialties of Archangel Gabriel include:

* Teaching
* Writing
* Childbirth
* Children
* Announcing new beginnings

Color Flame: copper light

A copper flame is an earth color and will ground you and protect you from any negativity. Visualize this copper energy from the earth coming up through your feet chakras up to your pelvic area or base of the spine. Then visualize your copper grounding cord going down to the center of the Earth and attaching there.

Gemstones: red tiger eye and hessonite garnet

Gemstone Meditation

Hold the red tiger eye or hessonite garnet in your left hand. Take a deep breath through your nose. Then release it quickly back through your nose becoming one with the gemstone. As you enter inside the gemstone, walk around and you will see different rooms. As you walk through the gemstone, on each door of each room you see a different subject title. While walking, you see the divine guidance room, the holistic natural remedy room, the nurturing room, and the healing room. You must decide now which room to go into. Whichever room you enter, Archangel Gabriel will be there to assist you in the healing process. Choose a room, and walk in; Archangel Gabriel is waiting for you to give you a message. He asks you to sit down and to ask your question. You begin asking him questions and receive answers. Be sure to listen to what he has to say. He explains to you how to listen to your inner child within and to your intuition. He places his copper light around you, nurturing you with divine love. You feel an overwhelming love come upon you and are very grateful and thankful to Archangel Gabriel. It is now time to return. Archangel Gabriel walks with you to the door of the gemstone and tells you he will be around you and to call on him at any time. You thank him. Then you open your eyes and come back to the present time, coming back into the room. You then release yourself from the gemstone by breathing in and out of your nose quickly.

Archangel Gabriel's Suggested Exercise

Place a journal next to your bed so when you have a dream you can write it down while it is fresh in your memory as you wake up. Another thing you can do is to record the dream into your cell phone microphone if you are not awake enough to write it down. This is a good exercise, according to Archangel Gabriel. Then during the day, you can look at what you have written or listen to your recording and interpret your dream. Ask Archangel Gabriel for help in interpreting your dream. Remember to listen to the recording or look at your journal after a few months have gone by to see how it has brought you useful information.

Another Exercise Suggested by Archangel Gabriel

Contact your inner child by going within, visualizing in meditation a small child playing alone. That child is you. Go up to the child, and see if she or he wants to play and if you can play together. Notice how the child is responding to you. Show the child love and that you want to join in and play with him or her. While doing this exercise, you will discover that your creativity and your abilities will come forth into your life and bring you a lot of fulfillment and happiness. Once you are finished with your inner child, take the child by the hand and bring him or her home within your heart. Love and acknowledge this child every day. Make an effort to do something creative and to nurture yourself daily.

Questions for Archangel Gabriel

* Can you bring me ideas to help me write this article?
* Can you help me decide on a name for my unborn child?
* Please help me to recognize opportunities and open doors that come into my life.

* While teaching others, can you bring me ideas to help them?

Message from Archangel Gabriel

Call on me, and I will help you to write down your thoughts and dreams in a journal. I will help you to make the right decisions by listening to your intuition. I will connect you with the right people at the right time. I will bring you the messages you need to know to live your best life. I will help you to listen to the inner child within and to your heart. Helping you to raise your children is a specialty of mine.

What is your heart and inner child telling you now? Make a list of things that would make your inner child happy, things you like to do for fun in your life.

1. _____
2. _____
3. _____

Archangel Haniel

Archangel Haniel is found not only in the Kabbalistic texts but also in the Babylonian texts. She assisted Enoch and carried him when he was translated into spirit. She is associated with the Ascended Master Maha Chohan, who brought the flame of the Holy Spirit upon Jesus Christ during the baptism of Jesus by John the Baptist. The Holy Spirit fell upon the disciples after Jesus Christ rose from the dead.

Maha Chohan now brings the flame of the Holy Spirit to humanity. He is in charge of the nature kingdom and the energy needed to perform supernatural miracles. In his last incarnation, he was a blind man named Homer. He was very creative and everybody was amazed at his speaking ability.

Specialties of Archangel Haniel include:

* Divine guidance through intuition
* Holistic natural remedies/gemstones
* Helping you to discern others' feelings
* Bringing you nurturing, loving energy
* Helping you to release things from your past
* Bringing harmony into your circumstances

Color Flame: pale blue and white

The pale blue color brings calmness and is very soothing to the physical body.

Gemstones: mother-of-pearl, moonstone, pearls, and chalcedony.

Gemstone Meditation

As you hold the gemstone of your choice, become one with the stone by taking a deep breath through your nose and releasing it quickly. Now you are within the gemstone, whether it be a moonstone, a pearl, or a mother of pearl. You can enjoy the atmosphere within the stone. Walk around within the stone; what do you see? How does it feel in there? Do you feel peaceful? How is the temperature in the gemstone? Is it warm? Cold? Do you hear anything? As you walk through the gemstone, express yourself freely through dance or song. This is a creative time for you to express yourself fully and to feel free. Operate from your heart and feel the love all around you. Visualize that your circumstances are coming into harmony. You are happy and joyful. All stress is dissolving within your life and you feel self-confident and strong. You realize that within the stillness a small inner voice is beginning to speak to you. As you get still and listen to your intuition, that inner voice speaks and gives you solutions to your problems. Your questions are being answered for you. Archangel Haniel is presenting solutions to your situation. She is very loving and brings down her nurturing energy around you. As you enjoy this presence of Archangel Haniel, you are very thankful. Now it is time to come back and release yourself from the gemstone. Archangel Haniel tells you that she will be with you to help you every day. You walk out of the gemstone, releasing yourself from it by breathing in through your nose and releasing the breath quickly out through your nose. You open your eyes and come back into the room.

Archangel Haniel's Suggested Exercise

Take a clear quartz crystal, and hold it in your left hand. Look at it carefully and see if you can see anything within the stone. Feel the energy of the crystal. How do you feel about that energy? Place the crystal out under the Moon in the evening, and leave it overnight to absorb the energy of the moon. In the morning, retrieve the crystal; then hold the crystal, and go into meditation, focusing on your third eye. Now look at the crystal once again and feel its energy. What is the crystal telling you? As you meditate with the crystal, let it speak to you. Pay attention to the thoughts that come into your mind. These are messages from the crystal communicating with you. Do this daily, and you will get to know your crystal's energy very well.

Questions for Archangel Haniel

* Can you assist me in my decisions to determine which alternative holistic health school I should attend?
* What alternative healing therapy should I be receiving?
* Can you show me which natural remedy I should be taking to benefit my health?
* I ask you for divine guidance on_____.
* What is my purpose in life?
* What do I need to know while making the decision about_____?

Message from Archangel Haniel

* Call on me, and I will send you loving, healing energy for difficult situations. I will help you feel good about yourself. I will help you with your studies of natural and alternative health. I will bring you divine guidance so you are able to discern your true purpose in life.

Can you think of anything in your past that you want to release, so you can move forward in life? Make a list of those items.

1. _____
2. _____
3. _____

Archangel Jeremiel

Archangel Jeremiel is found in the Judaic texts. He is considered one of the seven Archangels who brings to humanity prophetic visions. He also conducts the life review after death. He helps us to interpret our dreams for guidance. He is associated with the Ascended Master Lady Portia of mercy, kindness, grace, and fairness. She helps us to operate from the heart instead of from the mind, where we judge and criticize others. As we operate from the heart, we lift our vibration to a more loving state toward others and ourselves. She is on the Lords of the Karmic Board. Her symbol is the Maltese cross. When you need legal action, call on her.

Specialties of Archangel Jeremiel include:

* Developing psychic abilities
* Bringing us spiritual visions
* Reevaluating plans and goals
* Conducting a life review after death

Color Flame: dark purple-violet
Dark purple-violet is the color that heals the emotions. It brings spiritual awareness and spiritual protection for the aura. Place this purple-violet light over the white light bubble that you place over your aura.
Gemstone: amethyst

As you hold the amethyst in your hands, you are able to receive a purification and transmutation energy that will remove all negativity within your aura. It will open up your spiritual awareness and bring you into a higher consciousness state. This gemstone will allow you to meditate deeply while protecting you on a spiritual level from any negativity.

Gemstone Meditation

Place yourself in a relaxed state, and then focus on the amethyst in your hands. Notice the color and any variations within the stone. Feel the energy of the amethyst and how it feels in your hand. After focusing on the gemstone and feeling this energy, breathe through your nose, letting the breath out quickly, and becoming one with the gemstone. Now envision the gemstone becoming large as a house, now walk towards it and open the door to go in. Once you are inside, look around, and you will see a stairway that goes up to a special room. As you follow up the stairs and go into this room, you will find a divine spiritual being standing before you. Ask the question that you want to know of the divine being. Now listen for the answer. Once you receive the answer, thank the spiritual being and return down the stairs and out the door. Take a deep breath through your nose and let it out quickly, releasing yourself from the amethyst stone. Now open your eyes come back into the room, feeling good.

Archangel Jeremiel's Suggested Exercise

Place yourself in a relaxed state of mind. Close your eyes and begin to visualize and imagine that all your dreams have come true. Now look toward your past and view your memories and what you went through. This is called a life review within the life that you are living now. Ask yourself, how do I want to live the rest of my life? If you are happy with your past in this life, continue on your path to bring happiness. After examining your past through the life review, you are then able to make choices within your life to bring more satisfaction and happiness. By becoming aware of your thought patterns, you will be able to make changes to accomplish your goals and dreams.

Questions for Archangel Jeremiel

* How can I develop psychic abilities?
* Can you help me to clarify my goals?
* Show me what steps to take to achieve my goals.
* Which psychic ability do I have?
* Can you open up my psychic ability so I can see into my future?
* Help me to tune in and experience spiritual visions.
* What meditations can I do to bring me spiritual visions?

Message from Archangel Jeremiel

Call on me, and I will lift you up into a higher consciousness where you can receive spiritual visions and open yourself up to "clear seeing," or clairvoyance. This will enable you to help others when they come into difficulties in their life.

Archangel Jophiel

Archangel Jophiel is found in the Kabbalah texts in the Judaic tradition. She is also listed in the celestial hierarchy from the fifth century within the Christian tradition. She is all about beauty, creativity, and nurturing yourself. She is associated with the Ascended Master Kuthumi of wisdom, truth and love. In a past incarnation, Kuthumi worked with numerology, sacred geometry, and sound.

Specialties of Archangel Jophiel include:

* Helping you to get organized
* Helping you to clear clutter out of your life and your home
* Releasing negative people from your life
* Letting go of things you don't need anymore

Color Flame: golden yellow
Golden yellow is a color that stimulates the nervous system and the intellect. It brings wisdom, joy, and the connection to your higher self.

Gemstones: yellow sapphire, citrine, and yellow topaz

Gemstone Meditation

As you hold a citrine in your hand, quiet your mind and visualize a golden yellow light extending from the stone into your aura and around you. This will bring God's protection and wisdom to you to help you make better decisions in life. As you do this daily, God's protection and wisdom will increase, and you will easily be able to make decisions in your life and feel good about it. Make a conscious decision, and ask that you will be connected to your higher self or "I Am Presence." Archangel Jophiel will help you get organized if you clear out the clutter in your home or office.

Archangel Jophiel's Suggested Exercise

To clear out clutter in your home, do one room at a time. Obtain a large box, and place it in the room. Look at every item in the room, and ask yourself, "Does this item benefit me, and should I keep it?" If it does not benefit you, then place it in the large box within the room. After going through each item, you will make a decision to either throw the item away or keep it. Once you have placed items in the box, then you can donate them or throw them away. This is a simple way to clear out the clutter in your home. Once you do this, then you can organize the rest of the items within the room. The next step would be to Feng Shui each room in your house.

Questions for Archangel Jophiel

* I ask that you help me let go of all negative relationships in my life.
* Can you assist me in getting organized and clear the clutter out of my life?

* Can you bring positive people across my path to encourage me and help me in this life?

Message from Archangel Jophiel

Call on me when you want to get organized and are ready to clear out clutter and things within your home that you do not need anymore. I will also help you release negative people and relationships from your life. I can help with many situations that cause stress and negativity.

Archangel Metatron

Archangel Metatron is mentioned in the Judaic Kabbalah texts. Enoch, a man, ascended into the seventh heaven and became Archangel Metatron. He is associated with the Ascended Master Maha Chohan of the Holy Spirit Flame.

Specialties of Archangel Metatron include:

* Helping you to focus on owning your own personal power
* Healing past childhood traumas
* Helping you to set boundaries with others
* Helping you to get organized in your life
* Helping you to develop self-confidence
* Motivating you while focusing on your goals

Color Flames: green and violet

Green is a healing color and restores health on all levels. Violet is good for restoring and balancing the etheric body after shock, accident, or trauma.

Gemstone: watermelon tourmaline

Gemstone Meditation

As you meditate with the watermelon tourmaline, go within and focus on your breathing while placing yourself in a relaxed state of mind. Now visualize a pink-and-green light all around you and within your heart. Feel the love and the harmony that the light brings into your heart. While focusing on your heart, watch this pink-and-green light fill you up completely with unconditional love. Now send out this unconditional love to everyone you meet throughout the day. Continue to carry the watermelon tourmaline with you.

Archangel Metatron's Suggested Exercise

Become empowered and own your personal power by setting boundaries with people. Learn to say no and stand up for yourself. Watch yourself daily to see how many times you say yes to people and how many times you say no. If you say yes to people to please them, but you do not really want to do what they want you to do, be aware of that. Notice the emotions that come up with that situation of guilt or wanting to be accepted. Your goal here is to express who you really are without fear.

Questions for Archangel Metatron

* How can I increase my self-confidence so I can accomplish my goals and have better relationships?
* In dealing with other people and relationships, help me to say no.

* How can I focus on my goals and become motivated?
* Help me to feel better about myself and accept myself.
* Can you help me to forgive the things that happened to me in my childhood?
* Help me to become self-disciplined and organized in my life.
* How do I increase my personal power so I can feel better about myself?
* Can you help me to love myself, accept myself and express who I truly am?
* Can you help me to recognize my own personal power and setting boundaries with others?

Message from Archangel Metatron

Call on me to become organized and motivated while you focus on your goals and your priorities. I will surround you with loving, supportive people. I will help you to set boundaries with other people and to own your own personal power. You will be able to say no to others.

Archangel Michael

Archangel Michael is the Archangel of mercy in the Arabic tradition and in the Kabbalah within the Judaic tradition. He is in the apocryphal Book of Enoch. *"Michael, one of the holy angels, who, presiding over human virtue, commands the nations"* (Enoch 20:5).

"And Michael an angel from among the chiefs of the angels, took me by the right hand and lifted me up, and

led me out to all the secrets of mercy and to the secrets of justice. And he showed me all the secrets of the ends of heaven, and all the repositories of the stars and of the luminaries, and whence they proceed into the presence of the holy ones" (Enoch 71:3–4).

In the Christian tradition: "And there was war in heaven: Michael and his angels fought against the dragon; and the dragon fought and his angels, and prevailed not; neither was their place found any more in heaven. And the great dragon was cast out, that old serpent, called the Devil, and Satan, which deceiveth the whole world: he was cast out into the earth, and his angels were cast out with him" (Revelation 12:7–9 KJV).

Archangel Michael is associated with the Ascended Master El Morya of faith, truth, and protection. El Morya works with God's will, divine truth, and power. He is a member of the Great White Brotherhood. He works with the blue flame and the throat chakra. In his past incarnations, he was Abraham from the Bible, King Arthur from Britain, and one of the Tibetan holy ones. Call on him when you want to speak your truth and express your creativity according to God's will.

Specialties of Archangel Michael includes:

* Giving you courage and confidence to face difficult situations
* Removing demonic devices within your aura and body
* Clearing out negativity from your chakras and aura

- Cutting cords with negative people and energy vampires
- Pulling out poison arrows/negative thought forms
- Cutting you free from spirit attachments
- Releasing you from addictions by cutting the cords
- Fortifying your aura with strength and protection
- Sealing up tears, cracks, or holes in your aura
- Helping you to discover your life's purpose
- Repairing any mechanical and electrical items
- Placing shields around you for protection
- Clearing out a home, room, or office of negative energies
- Bringing you new opportunities and ideas in business
- Helping you to open jars and clasp necklaces

Color Flame: royal purple and cobalt blue

Royal purple is the color of transformation and higher consciousness. Cobalt blue is the color of protection, dissolving all negativity and helping an individual to express his or her truth.

Gemstones: lapis, amethyst, and sugilite

Gemstone Meditation

Hold your amethyst in your hand while placing yourself in a relaxed state. Meditate with the amethyst. Then place it on the area of your body where you need healing. Visualize the purple color going into the body where you feel pain. Then have it surround your aura so you are encased in a purple light. Visualize this purple light turning into a liquid and going throughout all the muscles of your body for pain relief. See Archangel Michael directing this purple light to absorb and dissolve all pain within your body.

Archangel Michael's Suggested Exercise

Visualize Archangel Michael standing before you, creating a force field shield of purple blue light around you for protection. This purple blue light fills your whole aura and fortifies it with strength and courage. Use this exercise when facing a difficult work situation or when you may be in danger. Other exercises with Archangel Michael will be covered in chapter seven concerning spiritual warfare techniques.

Questions for Archangel Michael

* Can you bring to my awareness what my purpose is to serve humanity?
* Can you send me protection as I drive and go throughout my day with your blue light?
* Can you clear out negative energies from my pet?
* Can you help me open this jar?
* Can you clear out all negative energies from my aura?
* Can you seal up all tears, cracks, and holes in my aura?
* Can you remove any spirit attachments that have attached onto my aura?

❋ Can you clear out any negative spirits that are in my house?

Message from Archangel Michael

Call on me for strength and courage to deal with any person or situation you are facing. I will cut you free from negative feelings of fear, depression, and anger with my golden sword of the Spirit. I will surround you with my blue flame of protection. I will direct you to your purpose in life and help you make decisions that will accomplish your goals according to God's will. You will know I am nearby by my sparkling purple-blue light. I will also help you with spiritual warfare when you are dealing with a psychic attack, negativity, or spirits.

Archangel Michael Healed my Car

I was coming home from work one day back in July 2010 when I stopped to get gas. It turned out that it was "bad" gas. It was raining that afternoon, and my car started to stall as soon as I drove it. I pulled into a nearby post office, and the engine stalled again. I did not think I would make it home. I got out of the car and checked the oil. Then I looked under my car on the driver's side and saw brown liquid leaking out. I got a Kleenex and dabbed it—brown oil. I checked the fluid levels, and they seemed okay. The car would not start again, and I knew it was not the battery because I had just gotten a new battery. It was getting dark. I lived only a couple of blocks down the street, but the next day was the Fourth of July and everything was going to be closed. I thought I was going to have to leave the car there and walk home in the rain.

Suddenly, I had the idea to call on Archangel Michael. There was no one else parked in the post office lot; I was alone. All of a sudden, a man appeared and walked up to my car, announcing that he was a mechanic. I told him the problem. He checked under the hood. I told him the car would not start and that there was a big puddle of oil underneath. He looked there, then under the hood again. He said everything was okay; I should just start the car and then drive home. I told him the car kept stalling and would not start. I did not believe him, and I did not want to be stuck in the middle of an intersection, stalled out.

He repeated himself three times, telling me to start the car and drive home, that everything would be fine. I thought I had better do what he said and hope for the best. I started my car and got home without stalling. I could not believe it! However, I knew I could not trust the car, since I had seen that brown oil gushing out. After the Fourth of July, I had the car towed to a mechanic and I explained what had happened. I even showed him the Kleenex with the brown oil on it as proof. The mechanics looked at the car and said there was no trace of any brown oil anywhere. That was impossible: there had been a huge puddle under the car.

Then I remembered I had called Archangel Michael for help because one of his specialties is fixing mechanical things. I thought again about the stranger appearing out of nowhere, walking up to the car and telling me it was okay to drive. After starting the car, I looked for the man, but he was gone. Could that have been an angel that Archangel Michael sent to me? I will never know. I do believe Archangel Michael and his angels healed the car. The mechanic said the car was totally fine and that there was nothing wrong with it. That seemed impossible to me, but I could not argue any more. Even if the rain had rinsed part of it away, oil and water do not mix, so there would have been at least a residue. I know it must have had something to do with bad gas, but it usually takes a while to clear that out. I never had any more problems with it.

How can Archangel Michael help you in your life? In my own life, there are many times where I do not have the strength to open a jar. I struggle on my own, but as soon as I ask Archangel Michael to come and help me, it immediately opens. Whatever I need to do around the house that requires strength or assistance, Archangel Michael helps by putting his hand on top of mine. Every time I need help, I call on him immediately. There is no reason to get upset because I cannot do something. I give him permission to help, and he does.

Make a list of the things you might need Archangel Michael to help you with, based on his specialties. Then work up the courage to call on him for help and give him permission to help you.

1. _____

2. _____

3. _____

Archangel Raguel

Archangel Raguel is found in the book of Enoch. *"Raguel, one of the holy angels, who inflicts punishment on the world and the luminaries"* (Enoch 20:4). He is associated with Ascended Master Lady Portia of justice, mercy, and grace.

Specialties of Archangel Raguel include:

* Healing arguments through forgiveness
* Bringing justice to those being manipulated or dominated
* Bringing opportunities to meet new people and develop new friendships

Flame color: light blue

Light blue is the color of peace and harmony and will resolve any misunderstandings within relationships. Light blue releases tension in the body.

Gemstones: aquamarine and blue topaz

Gemstone Meditation

Hold the aquamarine or blue topaz in your left hand. Now visualize becoming one with the gemstone as you breathe in through your nose and out your nose quickly. Now you are one with the gemstone and you find yourself walking along a path to a beautiful lake. You look up, and you see this gorgeous waterfall flowing down loudly into the lake, causing large ripples in the water. As you see the waterfall crashing down into the lake, it reminds you of your turbulent relationship and how difficult it is. All of a sudden, you feel the presence of an Archangel. Archangel Raguel is there standing beside you. He says, "As you still your mind and let the thoughts go, you will come into a state of harmony and peace within yourself and within your mind. Then you will be able to receive the answers to the difficult relationship you are in and know how to solve it." As you radiate the peacefulness from within, and express love into the relationship, you will find that all misunderstandings will be removed, and harmony will take its place in your life. You thank Archangel Raguel and start walking back down the path, realizing you now have some solutions for your relationship. Feeling happy and joyful, you take a deep breath through your nose and release it quickly, releasing yourself from the gemstone, opening your eyes, and coming back into the room.

Archangel Raguel's Suggested Exercise

Place yourself in a relaxed state, and still your mind. Now you will find yourself walking down a path to a beautiful place with birds singing and nature all around you. As you walk, you look at the different colors of the flowers and the trees rising tall above you in this magical place. As you come to this cottage with a golden door, you see crystals all around it and the door begins to open. You enter and find yourself in a comfortable, quiet room where there are chairs in a circle. You walk in and feel this peace, and you know you are there for a reason. As you sit down, Archangel Raguel walks into the room and greets you. Then he tells you that you can do an exercise to bring together the different parts of yourself. Being very intrigued, you want to know more. Archangel

Raguel explains that our selves have different parts, and those parts come into conflict. Problems are then created, preventing harmony within. Then we do not feel good about ourselves.

For example, you have an inner child that feels pushed aside and ignored. There is the judge, who wants to pass judgment, criticize, and make you feel you are not good enough. Then there is the priest who wants you to follow rules that others have imposed through the church to make you feel guilty or to control you. The rebel is stubborn and does not want to follow any rule. You have a physical body that is crying out for rest because it is being overworked. The workaholic comes in and says that you must survive. These are some of the parts of yourself that come to the forefront at different times to get their needs met.

Archangel Raguel continues: Let us look within. You will now see the different parts of yourself seated around this table in these chairs. Each part has an opinion that wants to be expressed within this setting. You, as the adult, must control the flow of the conversations that occur here. Let each one speak in turn. The inner child wants to speak now; listen to what the child has to say. Most likely, the child wants to play and go have fun and enjoy life, to take time out and do something new and adventurous. The workaholic wants to work and escape from the problems and does not have time for such unimportant activities. Then the physical body speaks and expresses the need for relaxation and feels it is being pushed too hard. The mind comes into play and wants something interesting to study and research. The emotions speak up and want to feel love and be in a relationship. As you let each part of yourself speak its opinion, solutions can be found. The different parts can negotiate and compromise with each other to bring balance within your lifestyle. When you feel that the different parts of yourself have agreed to work together in harmony to bring balance into your life, then you are done with the exercise.

Now take time to listen to the different parts of yourself. When you are done, thank Archangel Raguel for assisting in this process. It is now time to go back out of the cottage through the golden doors down the path. You feel good about bringing about harmony within yourself. As you walk down the path, take a deep breath through your nose and let it out; open your eyes and come back into the room. The purpose of this exercise is to recognize the needs of the different parts of yourself and to come to an agreement among all the parts, so you can have a more balanced lifestyle.

Questions for Archangel Raguel

* Can you help me to sort out and resolve any misunderstandings in my relationships?
* Can you bring me opportunities to meet new people and develop new friendships?
* Can you heal any arguments or misunderstandings that I have with my loved ones.

❧ Can you help me with self-confidence to stand up to others who may try to take advantage of me or control me?

Message from Archangel Raguel

Call on me and I will bring you friendships and business partners. I will open doors for you so you can move forward in achieving your goals. I would like to assist you in networking with other people and in bringing your product to market. I will help you to expand and develop new strategies for your business.

Archangel Raphael

Archangel Raphael is found in the Apocrypha in the book of Tobias. *"I am Raphael, one of the seven holy angels, which present the prayers of the saints, and which go in and out before the glory of the Holy One"* (Tobias 12:15).

He is also in the Kabbalah texts in the Judaic tradition. Archangel Raphael is also found in the book of Enoch. *"Raphael, one of the holy angels, who presides over the spirits of man"* (Enoch 20:3). *"The Lord said to Raphael, bind Azazyel hand and foot; cast him into darkness; and opening the desert which is in Dudael, cast him in there"* (Enoch 10:6).

Archangel Raphael is associated with the Ascended Master Hilarion, who is connected to healing, scientific knowledge and research. Hilarion focuses on the heart energy of love. He brings a person space and time to contemplate about what is important in life. In past incarnations, he was Paul the apostle.

Specialties of Archangel Raphael include:

* Physical healing
* Connecting you with your soulmate
* Exercise
* Emotional healing
* Sealing up your aura
* Helping you to love and forgive yourself
* Helping you to set boundaries with others
* Teaching you about holistic remedies
* Helping people to overcome addictions
* Protect you when you travel

Color flame: Emerald green
Emerald green is a very healing color and restores people's bodies to health.
Gemstones: emerald, fluorite, jade, and aventurine

Gemstone Meditation

As you hold Archangel Raphael's gemstone of your choice, close your eyes and take a deep breath through your nose; then breathe it out quickly. You will become one with the gemstone. Now the gemstone is getting as big as a house. You walk up to the door, and it opens for you. Walking inside, you see Archangel Raphael is waiting with his emerald-green light to heal and work with your aura. He has come to release any spirit attachments or entities from your aura and to escort them away from you. As he cuts any spirit attachments from your aura, he hands them over to Archangel Michael, who assists him in this process.

Archangel Michael and Archangel Raphael work as a team in spirit releasement and space clearing. After the spirits have been released and the negativity is removed from the aura, Archangel Raphael brings his emerald-green light of healing to heal the areas where the spirit attachments and negative thoughts have been removed from your aura. Then your aura is fortified with the blue-green light, and all cracks, holes, and tears in the aura are sealed up with the blue-green light. Now you are divinely protected. The process is complete. You walk back through the door, coming back to the here and now. You open your eyes, taking a deep breath through your nose and releasing yourself from the gemstone as you breathe out quickly. Feeling a sense of peace and happiness, you are thankful.

Archangel Raphael's Suggested Exercise: Pain Relief

Archangel Raphael is coming to heal your aura bringing the emerald-green light. Now he walks beside you as you both enter into your brain. You both become very small. When you walk in there and want to control the pain, go look at the dials. The dials go from one to ten. One is a very small amount of pain; ten is maximum pain. Turn the dials down to number one. Push the button and set it at number one. When you are finished, continue walking with Archangel Raphael. You find yourself with Archangel Raphael, walking along the beach. As you see your footprints in the sand, you continue to walk, and the waves come in and go out. As they come in to the shore, the waves flow over your footprints in the sand. As you watch, the waves go out to the ocean; the footprints dissolve, just as if your pain is being dissolved. As you continue to walk, you find yourself within your body at the place where there is pain. Archangel Raphael is there. He is saying, Let us communicate and ask the body what the problem is. What is the conflict? Why is there inflammation and pain in the neck (or whatever area needs attention)? Let us ask questions of that area. Why is there inflammation and pain in this area? The area replies: Because I am stuck in a rut and I am hesitant to change my ways. There is too much stubbornness here. The mind is closed to new ideas and afraid to take new risks. This area becomes inflamed and creates tension and pain because of fear. (It could be any message from the body. This is just an example.) Now Archangel Raphael sends the emerald green light of healing to that area of the body. You now realize what the problem is and why the body has pain and tension in that area. Now you can readjust your thinking patterns and take action, making some changes in your life. Now you understand your body.

How can Archangel Raphael help you in your life, with your health issues and lifestyle? After reading the above list of his specialties, create your own steps for your own healing process.

1. _____
2. _____
3. _____

"For an Angel went down at a certain season into the pool, and troubled the water: whosoever then first after the troubling of the water stepped in was made whole of whatsoever disease he had" (John 5:4 KJV).

"God sent me to heal thee, and to deliver Sarah, thy son's wife from the devil. For I am the Angel Raphael, one of the seven, who stand before the Lord." (Tobit 12:14–15, the Apocrypha).

"The holy angel of the Lord, Raphael was sent to heal them both, whose prayers at one time were rehearsed in sight of the Lord." (Tobit 3:25, the Apocrypha)

Questions for Archangel Raphael

* Can you show me and guide me into the right healing profession within the alternative health field?
* What can I do to lose weight?
* Can you help me make the right choices with my diet so I can lose weight?
* Can you bring me healing and restore my body to health?
* Which foods do I need to eat for increased health?
* How can I forgive and love myself?
* How can I recognize my addictions and how to eliminate them?
* Can you bring me protection while I travel?
* Can you help me to recognize my negative thinking patterns so I can change them to positive thinking?

Message from Archangel Raphael

I will help you forgive yourself and love yourself and others. Listen to your intuition, your feelings, and your heart for what you want in life. I will restore your body to health with my emerald-green light. I will help you to nurture and take care of your body through exercise, diet, and alternative health. I will bring love, joy, and laughter into your life. Call on me to bring my emerald-green light to you for healing.

Archangel Raziel

Archangel Raziel is found in the Kabbalah texts in the Judaic tradition. He knows the secrets of the universe, which include symbols, alchemy, seeing into the future, and divine magic. He also brings God's grace to humanity. He is associated with the Ascended Master Saint Germain of alchemy, healing, freedom, and the violet flame that dissolves all negativity. In his past incarnations, Saint Germain was Samuel the Prophet, Merlin the magician, Christopher Columbus, and the Count of Saint Germain. He traveled through Europe throughout the 1700s and never seemed to age. Saint Germain knew all the languages and became very knowledgeable and educated in science and the arts. He became immortal. His message was and still is to bring human consciousness into a higher consciousness of the higher self or divine self.

Specialties of Archangel Raziel include:

* Helping us to remember past lives
* Universal secrets/sacred geometry
* Helping us to interpret our dreams

Color Flame: indigo

The color indigo is related to the third-eye chakra and the pineal gland. It removes fears of the mind and insomnia and is very soothing as a pain reliever.

Gemstones: lapis lazuli and sodalite

Gemstone Meditation

Close your eyes, and bring yourself into a relaxed state of meditation. As you are lying down, place the lapis lazuli stone on your third eye between the eyebrows. Focus your attention on your third eye and relax. Let the thoughts come into your mind and go out without thinking about them. Focus now on your breathing. Continue to focus and be aware of your third-eye center. When you feel the energy of the stone, remove the lapis lazuli off your third-eye center and continue in meditation. As you go deeper in meditation, the mind becomes very quiet. Listen for the still, small voice within you. Ask a question in your mind and listen for the answer. When you are done, you can bring yourself back to the present time by counting one, two, three. Then open your eyes and come back into the room.

Archangel Raziel's Suggested Exercise

Place the white light of protection around yourself. Then place yourself in a relaxed state by breathing deeply and focusing on your breath. Just watch your breath as you breathe normally. Focus on your third eye and quiet your mind. Now ask a question of Archangel Raziel about the secrets of the universe and how it works. Ask him about the manifestation of your desires and dreams. Now wait and listen for any answers or information that may come into your mind. As you receive your answers and the information, you may want to write it down or record it into your cell phone to play back later. Be sure to give Archangel Raziel permission to bring you this information. Then thank him for the messages.

Questions for Archangel Raziel

* Can you help me to remember past events as I go into my past lives?
* In meditation, can you reveal universal secrets and information to me?
* Can you help me to discover what the messages are within my dreams?

Message from Archangel Raziel

As I assist you to travel back into your past lives, I will help you to remember them. As you go into a past life, I will assist you in healing your memories. I will also assist you in interpreting your dreams, which are used to deliver messages to you. I will forewarn you of things to come in your dreams.

Archangel Sandalphon

Archangel, Sandalphon is found in the Bible within the Christian tradition, as Elijah. *"And it came to pass, as they still went on, and talked, that, behold, there appeared a chariot of fire, and horses of fire, and parted them both asunder; and Elijah went up by a whirlwind into heaven "* (2 Kings 2:11 KJV). He now resides as Archangel Sandaphon in the Judaic tradition within the Kabbalah mystical texts. You may feel his presence of inspiration and receive new ideas for songwriting as you attune to him and call on him for help. You may see a sparkling turquoise light when he comes near. He will enhance your creativity and talent within the music arena. Before performing your music be sure to call on him to enhance the healing aspect of the sounds, which will reach your audience with a love frequency.

He is associated with the Ascended Master Mother Mary of divine love and service. Her specialties are love and devotion.

Specialties of Archangel Sandaphon include:

- Delivering your prayers and requests up to God, so they can be answered
- Assisting you with your creativity as you write songs and music.
- Bringing you new ideas for writing music.
- Assisting you while you perform, playing your musical instrument.
- Enhancing and increasing your talent within the music industry.
- Transmitting healing through your music.
- Healing and soothing those who are angry or aggressive.

Color flame: turquoise

The color turquoise is a very healing and soothing color, which brings strength to the physical body. It corresponds to the throat chakra and the thyroid gland. It enhances our creativity, and our self-expression.

Gemstone: turquoise

Gemstone Meditation.

As you hold the turquoise stone in your hand, you will feel its soothing vibration. As you breathe deeply you start receiving messages within your mind. You listen intently, begin to sense, and see the words coming into your mind. Then symbols appear before you within a mist of turquoise color. Archangel Sandalphon then appears and tells you what the symbols mean for your life. The Archangel reveals how the color turquoise revitalizes you and strengthens your aura. This turquoise color will also protect you from negativity as the Archangel continues. After you bathe in this beautiful turquoise light, you feel the stone in your hand. As you breathe in and out, you become alert and open your eyes.

Archangels Sandalphon Suggested Exercise.

Place yourself in a relaxed state of mind. Now visualize yourself stepping into a beautiful pool of turquoise water glistening with turquoise light. As you step into this pool, you feel invigorated and youthful. Saturated by the water you feel happy. Then you look through this clear turquoise water, and you see your future self, who has already achieved and is living your dreams in the future. After seeing these pictures within your vision the ideas have now been imprinted in your mind's eye. Now all you have to do to create and activate these dreams for yourself is to talk about, focus on, and act on your dreams. As you feel the excitement building up within you, you step out of the turquoise water, becoming alert and coming back into the room.

Questions for Archangel Sandalphon

* Can you show me how to pray to God for Him to hear my prayers?
* Can you help me write songs on healing so others can become attuned to the higher frequencies of love and light?
* Can you bring me ideas for writing music that can be used for healing the physical, emotional, and mental energies within others and myself?
* I need your assistance in learning this musical instrument. Can you help me?
* Please help me to speak out the promises of God to activate my faith so God will respond and answer my prayers.

Message from Archangel Sandalphon

Call on me, and I will take your prayers and concerns up to God. You can be sure they will be heard and God will respond with loving kindness. For God loves you and will always bring a solution to whatever problem you are facing. Be patient and always place your faith in God.

Archangel Uriel

Archangel Uriel is found in the book of Enoch. *"Uriel one of the holy angels, who presides over clamour and terror"* (Enoch 20:2). Also in the Kabbalah mystical texts, he is found. *"Unto these things Uriel the Archangel gave them answer, and said, even when the number of seeds is filled in you: for he hath weighed the world in balance"* (2 Esdras 4:36 in the Biblical Apocrypha KJV). He is associated with the Ascended Master Jesus Christ, Lord of the red ray, the Son of God who was resurrected from the dead. Jesus Christ represents divine love, truth, and life. Archangel Uriel is also associated with the Ascended Master Lady Nada of divine love and service. Her specialties are healing, devotion, and enlightenment. Her message is that there should be love and wisdom together. In past incarnations, some believe she was Mary of Magdala.

Specialties of Archangel Uriel includes:

* Memory problem-solving
* Bringing new ideas to you as you speak or write
* Helping you to remember information when you are taking a test.
* Heals bitterness and resentment

Color Flame: yellow, gold, and purple light

Gold is the color of prosperity. It connects you up with your higher God self. Purple helps you to meditate and brings you into a higher consciousness. The color yellow will remove any fear that may come up for you in life.

Gemstones: golden amber, yellow fluorite, and golden topaz

Gemstone Meditation

As you hold the yellow fluorite in one hand and the golden amber in the other, you will unify and balance yourself to receive a higher consciousness free from fears. As you look at these gemstones in your hands take a deep breath through your nose, release it quickly, and become one with the gemstones. Now close your eyes and visualize the yellow light from the yellow fluorite expanding from the gemstone and filling your aura, removing all fear and anxiety. Now visualize the golden light from the golden amber expanding from that gemstone and filling up your aura with golden light merging with the yellow light. This light flows to your third eye and up your crown chakra, up to your higher self, which is a golden color. The "I Am Presence", which is your God self or higher self, will bring you into a state of higher consciousness. Continue to place your attention on your higher self of golden light. Now bring that golden light energy of your higher self into your physical being; feel it merging with your body. Now this golden energy is radiating out from your aura, and you become the golden light. Enjoy the presence of the golden light being one with everything and the universe. This is an expanding energy of freedom and higher consciousness. Enjoy this moment. When you are ready to come back visualize yourself coming back to the present time in this reality by counting from one to three. As you take a deep breath through your nose and let it out quickly, release yourself from these gemstones. You are now back in the present time in this reality. You may open your eyes and come back into the room.

Archangel Uriel's Suggested Exercise

When you need to do research and study, call on Archangel Uriel to help you understand what you are studying. He will give you insights and new ideas as you study and learn. Quiet your mind, close your eyes, and focus on your third eye. Place yourself in a relaxed state. Take deep breaths in and out. Now focus on your normal breathing. You can begin to ask questions of the Archangel. Listen for the answers in the silence. Give him permission to speak to you, and he will speak into your mind, bringing you knowledge that you did not have before. As his thoughts come into your mind, speak them out into your cell phone recorder or write them down in your journal. He will instruct you. When you are ready to return to normal consciousness, you can bring yourself back by counting from one to three, taking a deep breath in with your nose, and letting it out. Open your eyes and come back into the room in the present time.

Questions for Archangel Uriel

* Can you send me new ideas so I can solve problems in my life?
* Can you help me to study and remember the information so I can pass the test?
* Can you guide me to the research I need to complete for writing these articles?

Message from Archangel Uriel

I will bring you creative ideas for solving your problems. Be sure to follow the guidance I give you and act on the ideas that you receive in your mind from me. I will help you with your school studies and with your memory when you are taking a test. I will give you the wisdom to make the right decisions.

What are the problems that you need solutions for? Quiet your mind and ask Archangel Uriel for ideas. Then listen. As you receive ideas, write them down on a piece of paper. Follow the advice and take action. Be sure to give Archangel Uriel permission to bring you the ideas that you need. Thank him for the ideas you have received.

Archangel Zadkiel

Archangel Zadkiel is found in the Kabbalah mystical texts. He is also known as Archangel Sachiel and Tsadkiel. He is associated with the Ascended Master Saint Germain of healing, the violet flame and freedom. The violet flame will dissolve and transform all negative energy into a higher vibration. Saint Germain never aged and ascended in the late 1800s. He influenced men to promote freedom. He taught others to access their higher self through the techniques of alchemy for the transformation of consciousness to a higher level.

Specialties of Archangel Zadkiel include:

* Healing painful memories/Helping you to forgive yourself and others
* Dissolving and transforming all negativity
* Self-acceptance and confidence
* Improving memory

Flame color: indigo blue to purple-violet
Indigo blue and purple-violet increase intuition and are calming colors; they relieve pain.

Gemstones: lapis, amethyst, purple fluorite, and sodalite

Gemstone Meditation

Place the amethyst in your left hand. Now close your eyes, take a deep breath in through your nose, and breathe it out quickly through your nose, becoming one with the amethyst. Now visualize the amethyst becoming as big as a house. You are walking along a path and you see beautiful flowers and birds singing and trees up ahead. As you continue, you reach an amethyst-crystal house; you walk inside, seeing a beautiful purple violet color all around you. There are many doors leading to different rooms. You walk up to one door that says Forgiveness. Then you walk to another door that says Self-Acceptance. As you continue to walk and look at the different doors, you see a door that says Healing. You proceed to walk through the door into this room. You find Archangel Zadkiel is there, waiting for you. He tells you to go in, sit down, and relax. There is a TV screen in front of you. All of a sudden, you see scenes from your past where forgiveness was needed to be given but was not.

Archangel Zadkiel asks you to forgive and send love to those people who hurt you in the past. When you forgive them, the memories of the hurts will be healed within you. It does not mean that you have forgotten what was done, but you are releasing that person from your energy field by forgiving them. As you forgive them by speaking, all hurt and pain starts dissolving in the purple-violet light. This healing purple-violet light fills you completely, dissolving all negativity in and around you, bringing a spiritual awareness to you. You feel so good and self-confident now that you have released those people from your life. You feel free and know that healing is yours. Now you see the violet purple light come down, bringing calmness and increased intuition. You can see clearly now. Archangel Zadkiel tells you that the healing is completed; the painful memories have been dissolved and healed. It is now time to return to the present. Archangel Zadkiel says that you can call on him for help. He will be with you. You thank him, and start back by walking out the door of this beautiful amethyst crystal house and walking along the path. Passing the flowers, trees, and birds singing, you continue to walk and come back to the present time. By taking a deep breath and letting it out quickly, you release yourself from the amethyst and find yourself opening your eyes and coming back into the room.

Archangel Zadkiel's Suggested Exercise

Call on Archangel Zadkiel to come. He is now standing beside you and wants to show you something. You find yourself at the beach, walking down a stairway to the sand and the waves. As you walk along the sand on the beach, you see a child in the distance. It is you, as your inner child. Archangel Zadkiel asks if you would like to greet the child. The child is a part of you—you can play together. You watch the child and see what she is doing. She is painting, being very creative and free. You created art when you were younger, the Archangel tells you. You stopped, and your creativity has gone down; the child is very sad and very lonely. He invites you to go entertain the child and talk with her. You walk closer: She appears to be eight to ten years old. You ask what she is making.

She says she is painting different colors, and they are pretty. She loves the colors and loves to paint. You decide to go with her and create art together, exploring the different colors. Then the child becomes a spiritual being and merges one with you—for the child is a part of you. You feel love and joy within. Archangel Zadkiel walks with you back along the beach and up the stairs. Now you are back in the present time as you open your eyes and come back into the room, feeling loved and appreciated.

Questions for Archangel Zadkiel

* Can you heal my painful memories from the past and from my childhood?
* Can you help me to forgive myself and other people?
* Will you bring the purple violet light to transmute and dissolve all negativity within my home?
* Can you help me to enhance my memory?
* Can you help me to remember the important things I need to remember throughout the day?
* Will you dissolve all negativity within my aura?
* Can you transform all negative situations into positive situations?

Message from Archangel Zadkiel

I will bring the violet flame to transmute and dissolve all painful memories of the past. I will bring love to help you to forgive yourself and others. Call on me to cleanse and transmute all negativity in any situation or environment. You will discover who you are and accept yourself completely with love as I shower down my love upon you. I will help you release old habits and patterns of the past.

Is there anyone you can think of that you may need to forgive? Think back into your past and make a list. Forgiving does not mean forgetting a past wrong; it means that you are just releasing the negative emotions associated with a particular person or situation. You are freeing yourself from the negativity, and you are releasing it to God and letting Him take care of the situation.

People or situations that need forgiveness.

1. _____
2. _____
3. _____

How do you Ask for Help and Contact an Archangel?

* Say,"I call on Archangel ___, and I give you permission to help me."
* Ask your question.
* Be specific in your request.
* Thank the Archangel for his services.
* Follow the guidance and/or take decisive action.
* Listen to your intuition; it may be a message.

How To Know If An Archangel Is Sending You A Message

* The Archangels often speak to us through intuition.
* You may receive new ideas as flashes of insight.

❋ You may feel warmth in your body and feel at peace.

❋ You may see sparkling, colored lights around you.

❋ You may see a physical manifestation of an Archangel.

❋ Strangers can deliver unexpected messages; be open to them.

❋ You may see an Archangel in your dream.

❋ Thoughts will come into your mind that you do not recognize as your own.

❋ You may see a colored orb of light.

What do you want to accomplish in your life? Can you remember when you were a child, what you liked to do and what you wanted to be when you grew up? What are your dreams and passions? Can you list them?

1. _____

2. _____

3. _____

4. _____

Summary

We end this chapter on the Archangels and their specialties as well as the Ascended Masters who are associated with each Archangel. I hope you now have a better idea about which Archangel and Ascended Master to call on for your particular problem. The Archangels are loving beings who are directed by God to give us divine guidance. The angels are here not to interfere with our free will but to help us act according to God's will. Never worship angels—only worship God. God sends angels to help us.

CHAPTER 6

UNDERSTANDING THE TOOLS ARCHANGEL MICHAEL USES IN SPIRITUAL WARFARE

———

Behold, I give unto you power to tread
on serpents and scorpions, and over
all the power of the enemy: and nothing
shall by any means hurt you.

—LUKE 10:19 KJV

And there was war in heaven: Michael
and his angels fought against the dragon;
and the dragon fought and his angels,
and prevailed not; neither was their
place found any more in heaven.

—REVELATION 12:7–8 KJV

In the last chapter, we talked about the Archangels' specialties. In this chapter, we are going to talk about the tools and techniques that the Archangels use for spiritual warfare and healing. We will describe each tool or technique used to clear out negativity and for healing.

Clearing and Healing Tools of the Archangels

Have you ever wondered how Archangel Michael battles and overcomes evil? The Archangels have tools and techniques for spiritual warfare, and for healing situations. Archangel Michael uses tools in spiritual warfare, while Archangel Raphael uses tools of healing. These two Archangels often work as a team. Archangel Michael clears out and cuts us free from negative cords, and then Archangel Raphael will bring healing to those areas where the cords have been cut with his emerald-green light.

Archangel Michael's Tools and Techniques

Archangel Michael has a cobalt blue flame of protection. Visualize a blue light that surrounds you and forms a bubble around your aura to protect you from all negativity.

Archangel Michael has a golden sword of the spirit. Call on him and ask him to use it to cut all negative cords that have been attached to you by other people.

Archangel Michael has a magnet that can pull out all poison arrows, or negative thought forms, from your aura. Call on him, and ask him to use his magnet to pull out all negative thought forms.

He also carries large pruning shears—he can use these to cut you free from all spiritual chains that have been wrapped around you to create limitations and to keep you from expressing yourself. Call on Archangel

Michael to cut and remove any limiting chains that have been placed around you to hold you back.

Archangel Michael also has a spiritual vacuum. He uses it to clear out and cleanse each chakra and to pull out all negative energy. Visualize him using it for increased health. Archangel Michael has a long tube to remove all entities and attachments from you. Call on him, and give him permission to remove all spirit attachments or entities that have attached to your aura.

Have Archangel Michael use his large wrench to remove and dismantle all spiritual armor that has been placed over you or around you.

Ask Archangel Michael and Archangel Raphael to use their large spiritual caulking spatula to seal up any tears, cracks, or holes in your aura.

Ask Archangel Raphael to use his emerald-green light to heal the areas where the negative cords have been cut and where the poison arrows or negative thought forms have been removed.

Ask Archangel Raphael to use his paintbrush and different colors to make each of your chakras bright, beautiful, and healthy—after Archangel Michael has vacuumed them out and cleared them of dark, negative energy. Archangel Raphael can also use a spray gun of color for the chakras after Archangel Michael cleanses them.

Other Tools of Spiritual Warfare

* By faith use Jesus Christ name, authority, and blood to protect you against all negativity. This will work if you are a believer.

* Bind spirits in Jesus Christ name to deactivate their power. There are spirits of depression, fear, pain, and criticism—that can affect us.
* Use Ascended Master Saint Germain's violet flame to clear a room, person, or situation. Call on Saint Germain to bring his violet flame; this will burn up and dissolve all negativity. Be sure to place a white light within the area before you visualize the violet flame. The white light is from the Holy Spirit bringing unconditional love and purity. The violet flame will remove and dissolve all negativity.
* Use a white light to protect you from physical harm and as an overall protection for your aura.
* Place a purple light over the white light to protect you against negative spirits.
* Release all excess and foreign energy, all pain and stress, down into the earth to be transformed into love, light, and blessing by Mother Earth. Give thanks to Mother Earth.
* Call the Angelic Host to bring down the sacred fire of love and perfection into any situation.
* Call on the Ascended Masters and higher beings of light for help and assistance.
* Use the cosmic blue lightning fiery flame of Christ to protect you or an environment.
* Call on your Mighty I AM Presence or higher self to come down into your personality and spiritual body to bring about a higher consciousness.
* Speak the word of God in the name of Jesus Christ.
* Command all spirits to go to the second dimension in the name and authority of Jesus Christ.

* Send ghosts into the light with the assistance of the Archangels and Jesus Christ name.
* Visualize a pink light shield that will protect you against negativity, complaining, and gossipy people. Only allow love to come in.
* Call on your Guardian Angel for protection and to watch over you while you are driving and generally throughout your day.
* Visualize copper energy coming up through the bottom of your feet and into your body; ask it to remove all negative energy from you.
* Visualize silver light to redirect another person's negative energy away from you.

The best tool against a psychic attack or an energy vampire is to place protection techniques around yourself every morning, and then to call on Archangel Michael for protection. If you keep your chakras cleared out and you are protected, you will be less likely to be affected by negativity. The color green will protect you against a psychic attack.

Ask yourself, do you protect your aura, clean out your chakras and ground and run your energy daily?

In this chapter, we discussed the tools used in spiritual warfare. In the next chapter, we will talk about how to use these tools in everyday situations.

CHAPTER 7

LEARNING HOW TO USE THE TOOLS OF SPIRITUAL WARFARE OF ARCHANGEL MICHAEL, JESUS CHRIST, AND SAINT GERMAIN

———

And the seventy returned again with joy, saying, Lord, even the devils are subject unto us through thy name.

—LUKE 10:17 KJV

Behold, I give unto you power to tread on serpents and scorpions, and over all the power of the enemy: and nothing shall by any means hurt you.

—LUKE 10:19 KJV

In the last chapter, we discussed and learned about spiritual warfare tools and what they are. In this chapter, we will cover how to use the tools of spiritual warfare that belong to Archangel Michael, Jesus Christ, and the

Ascended Master Saint Germain. We will also cover how to use the colored flames in different situations in everyday life.

Tools of Spiritual Warfare and How to Use Them

Have you ever walked into an empty room and immediately felt depressed or angry? It is because people who are depressed or angry left their negative energies behind. How can we apply the tools of Saint Germain, an Ascended Master, Archangel Michael, and Jesus Christ in spiritual warfare in our daily lives to remove and protect ourselves from negative energy?

To Clear a Room, Office, or Home of Negativity

To clear a room of negativity, first visualize white light going through the room and filling every area of it. Then call on Saint Germain, and give him permission to bring in his violet flame. Work methodically through the whole room, visualizing the violet flame burning up and dissolving all negativity within that room. When Saint Germain is done, visualize the white light of the Holy Spirit going through the whole room once again. Now call on Archangel Michael to bring his blue light of protection into the room; cover every area of it. Be sure to give your permission for Archangel Michael and Saint Germain to help you and bring in their colored flames. Then call on Archangel Raphael to bring his emerald-green light into the room, filling it with peace and harmony. This is a standard technique for clearing out negativity and for harmonizing a room, home, or office. Clearing out spirits and ghosts is a more involved process that is covered in future chapters.

Cutting Negative Cords with Archangel Michael

A cord is a link that connects two people on a spiritual level. Cords can be positive or negative. A positive cord links two people in love and friendship. A negative cord links two people in a power struggle or allows an energy vampire to drain the other person's energy. Cords are usually attached to different chakras that correlate to different types of energy. A power-struggle cord would connect solar plexus to solar plexus, for example; the solar plexus is our personal power center in our chakra system. A cord of love would connect from heart to heart.

Wherever you go, people will attach energy cords to your chakras. When you enter a room and talk with strangers or even just meet up with friends, it is possible you will pick up their energies and emotions—if you are not protected. They could drain your energy, which would make you feel depressed after talking with them. This is why it is good for us to protect ourselves before we go out of the house in the morning. After our workday is finished, it is also good to clear ourselves of all foreign and excess energy by cutting the negative cords with all the people we met throughout the day. Archangel Michael can assist us with this. He will cut the cords with his golden sword of the spirit. When he is done, you will receive your energy back and feel strong again.

We can pray for people, but it is best not to try to take on another person's problems—if their energy is not compatible with ours, it will disrupt our own energy fields. Even if you feel you are compatible with a person because he or she is a friend, remember that each person is unique and vibrates at a certain frequency. If you do not clear another person's energy from your own after interacting, it can create problems for your own energy field and stop it from functioning well. It is best to send another's energy back to him or her with a blessing and love.

Call on Archangel Michael and give him permission to cut all negative cords between you and other people with his golden sword of the Spirit. Once he cuts the cords, visualize the cords coming back to you and going back to the other person. Then ask Archangel Raphael to come in with his emerald-green light to fill up the areas in your aura where the cords have been cut, to heal them.

Removing Poison Arrows from Your Aura

What is a poison arrow? A negative thought form that a person sends you. Sometimes someone sends one to hurt you intentionally, but other times people do not even realize they are sending them. Whenever a person expresses negative thoughts and emotions, they can lodge themselves in your aura if you are not protected. That is again, why it is very important to protect yourself and have a detached attitude before you walk out the door in the morning. If we recognize that talking to a certain person makes us angry or depressed, we can choose not to accept that energy; we can send it right back, with a blessing.

Do this in your mind as you are talking to someone. Visualize a white light bubble of the Holy Spirit around you for protection. Layer purple light over the white light bubble, and then layer blue light over that purple light. This will protect you during the conversation. At the end of your day, release all excess and foreign energy, all pain and stress down into the earth. Mother Earth will transform it into love, light, and blessing. Be sure to give thanks to Mother Earth afterward! Then call on Archangel Michael and give him permission to draw all negative thought forms from your aura with his magnet. Visualize him circling your aura with his magnet, removing all of them. Next, call on Archangel Raphael and give him permission to bring his emerald-green light of healing to fill up the areas where the negative thought forms have been removed in your aura. Call on both Archangel Raphael and Archangel Michael to fortify your aura with their blue and emerald-green lights.

Clearing Out and Cleansing Each Chakra

Call on Archangel Michael and give him permission to come and "vacuum out" each of your chakras by drawing out negative energy. Start by envisioning your root chakra, then move upward, stopping at each chakra. Ask him to remove all the negative and dark energy from each chakra. Then call on Archangel Raphael to come in with healing and to spray each chakra with its color to make it bright and beautiful again. After this is done, your chakras will be healthy and clean. As Archangel Michael finds any entities or spirit attachments on your aura, he will use a long tube to suck and remove them.

Released entities are then directed to a place where they can be guarded by the angels until God can redirect them to where they are supposed to be. If you keep your chakras cleared out and you protect yourself each day, you will feel peaceful and positive.

Sealing Up Tears, Cracks, and Holes in Your Aura

Although you may have been practicing protecting yourself, running your energy, grounding your energy, and generally strengthening your aura with meditation, it is still possible for your aura to be damaged by negative energy. Call on Archangels Michael and Raphael, and give them permission to seal up any tears, cracks, or holes in your aura with their "spiritual spatulas." They can smooth out your aura just as we would smooth plaster. They will patch these damaged areas with their blue and emerald-green lights. Visualize this process as you call on them. This technique should be used after Archangel Michael has cut all negative cords and removed any poison arrows from your aura.

Removing Armor with Archangel Michael

Archangel Michael has a large screwdriver he can use to remove and dismantle the demonic spiritual armor that has been placed on parts of your body, by the demonic forces to limit you. Ask Archangel Michael to go ahead and remove any armored plates he sees. Usually, while you are in meditation, you will be able to see armor on your body. Archangel Michael also uses large scissors like pruning shears to cut any chains that have been placed around your neck or around your body, creating limitations for you, or stopping you from expressing your true self.

The Ultimate Protection: The Blood of Christ

The blood of Christ is the most powerful weapon available for spiritual warfare. Jesus Christ died and shed his blood for our sins, and after three days, he rose again and overcame death and the Devil. To apply the blood by faith is very powerful. You must truly believe that Jesus Christ is the Son of God and that the Bible is true for this to work. If you believe, have received Christ into your heart, and have made Christ the Lord of your life, you will be able to use his blood to overcome all negativity and evil. This is called pleading the blood. By faith, you can say, I plead the blood of Christ over my mind, over my heart, and over my body in Jesus Christ name. This will protect you from all negativity and evil. Faith is activated by believing in what you say aloud. You can plead the blood over a situation or person, over your car, or even over your home. No evil will be able to touch you when the blood has been applied. There is power in the blood. It is best to do this every morning and night before you go to sleep.

Binding Spirits and Commanding Them to Go

You can bind spirits and command them to go to the second dimension in Jesus Christ name and by his authority. You can also call Archangel Michael to come and get any unwanted spirits. He will take them to a holding place until God redirects them to where they are supposed to be. Once again, you must be a believer in Jesus Christ, and he must be your Lord for this to work. The spirits will obey if the speaker uses the name of Jesus Christ and his authority through his power and blood. If you have not accepted Christ as your savior, I advise you not to try using this technique, simply because it will not work for you.

Can you deal with your own negative feelings in spiritual warfare? Yes, you can bind the anger or jealousy in and around you. The important thing is to bind it before it consumes you. Put your focus on Jesus Christ and plead the blood of Christ over yourself. Then speak out a Bible verse that is related to your situation. For example, *"For God hath not given us the spirit of fear; but of power, and of love, and of a sound mind" (2 Timothy 1:7 KJV).* You are acting as an authority through God's word; you are addressing the situation in Jesus Christ name. Call on Archangel Michael and give him permission to come and assist you.

Using the Colored Flames

Call on Saint Germain and Archangel Zadkiel and give them permission to bring the violet flame down to burn up and consume all negativity around you. They can dissolve it and transmute it into love and light. Visualize this violet flame to clear a room, person, or situation. Be sure to place the white light of the Holy Spirit around that person or situation or throughout a room before applying the violet flame.

The cosmic-blue lightning fiery flame of the Christ can be used for protection and to transmute any negativity within a room or a situation.

You can also use the pink light shields to protect against negativity, complaining, or gossipy people. The pink flame brings unconditional love into any situation or to any person.

Call on your Mighty "I Am Presence" or higher self to come down into your personality and spiritual body to bring about a higher consciousness. As your higher self comes into your personality and physical body, you will be more protected, as you will be vibrating on a higher frequency. To raise your frequency level, you can also speak out the word of God in the name of Jesus Christ. As you speak the word, it opens up the supernatural, and miracles will occur. The angels will then draw near to you, and you will feel the presence of God within and around you.

Calling on the Angelic Host

Call on the Angelic Host and give them permission to bring down the sacred fire of love and perfection into your situation. This will bring peace and resolve any difficult situation. The Angelic Host can work on any issue or problem. The Angelic Host includes the Ascended Masters and the angels—they work as a team for the Almighty God.

Spiritual Warfare at Work: My Story

I once had a job where the manager was very abusive to everyone. She would threaten to fire us every day. It was very harsh, and she worked us like dogs. My assessment of her was that she had more than one personality and that she had multiple spirit attachments. She was full of criticism and jealousy, and she wanted attention all the time—to the point of ignoring customers. I would call in Archangel Michael to protect me before I went into work every day. I also performed my usual protection techniques in the morning and pleaded the blood of Jesus Christ over me. When the abuse got severe, I turned to other spiritual warfare techniques. Before I would go to work, I would cleanse the workplace with white light, the violet flame, the blue-lightning flame of Jesus Christ, and the blue flame of Archangel Michael. I called on the Angelic Host to bring down their sacred fire of love and perfection. I bound the spirits around the manager in Jesus Christ name, and I told them they could not speak when I was around.

Thanks to my doing all these things, she would criticize my coworkers but not me. Before I bound the spirits in Jesus Christ name, she would criticize me as well. Afterward, she left me alone. This really does work.

One day she came at me, but when she got close, she actually bounced back, because she felt a force field around me. She asked, "What was that?" I told her it was Archangel Michael standing in front of me. She was a Catholic and knew about the Archangels, so she was amazed. I knew that I had been led there to be trained by God in spiritual warfare techniques. I learned a great deal during that difficult time—I was there about nine months.

When I started clearing out the workplace with the colored flames of the Archangels and the violet flame before I started my shift, I noticed something: whenever I would come in to work, the manager would say she had to leave. It was only three o'clock in the afternoon, and she was scheduled to be there until five, but she would make up some excuse. The energy was of a higher vibration, and the spirits that were attached to her simply could not stay in that place. I would clear the workplace out right before I got to work.

During this difficult time, I learned how to bind spirits in Jesus Christ name. I also learned how to call on Archangel Michael and have him stand before me to repel the negativity.

I have worked in retail since 1986, and this was the worst case of dysfunction and abuse I had ever seen. Nobody could handle it. All the employees walked away except for one girl, who had no choice but to stay. She believed she could not get any other job, for some reason. I knew I was meant to be there to practice what I had learned. I taught the other girl the techniques I was using so she could survive. I would bind the spirits of fear, aggression, abusiveness, anger, and jealousy around my manager. After many months on the job, the manager came running up to me one day and said she needed help.

"Which angel was that again that you always call on?" she asked.

I told her it was Archangel Michael. We called on him for protection, and I visualized the light of Christ and Archangel Michael's blue light around her, to clear out her negative spirits in Jesus's name. I was only an instrument—Jesus Christ and the angels were doing the real work.

It took eight months of spiritual warfare, but eventually the woman changed completely—from a vicious person to one who was asking for help. She still had multiple personalities, but she was 100 percent better in her behavior. I really believe that she had spirits attached to her and possibly within her. There was definitely a demonic stronghold on her that was too much for me to try to cast out alone. Before I started binding the spirits attached to her, she would complain and criticize us in a particular, whining voice, but after I bound the spirits in Jesus Christ name, I noticed her voice changed back to normal. It was as if the second personality had just disappeared. It was amazing to me. This is how I know spiritual warfare does work and is real. I learned a lot from that experience. I was tested, and I put the spiritual warfare tools to use—with Jesus Christ help, they worked. I have to say, it changed the place. Four months after I left, the company fired the manager. She was going against policies of the company and was dishonest to boot. Even the regional manager was fired because she had not been able to keep her in check.

Now, if I come across a person who is angry, jealous, arrogant, selfish, depressed, or fearful, I will immediately bind the spirits attached to him or her. It stops that person from affecting me. Negativity bounces right off me. Archangel Michael protects me. Saint Germain burns up any negativity around me with his violet flame. Jesus Christ protects with his lightning-blue flame. The Angelic Host brings down the sacred fire of love and perfection.

In spiritual warfare, if you call on the Archangels for help, plead the blood of Jesus Christ, and call on the authority and power of God to defeat and overcome any negative circumstances, problems, or spirits. This is the only way to overcome the demonic forces, principalities, and powers. Remember that we are dealing with the spiritual realms and that everything that comes into this physical plane exists first in the spiritual realm. Many of our problems are rooted in the spiritual realms; they simply manifest in the physical realms. You cannot correct most situations and problems by trying to reason your way out of them or trying to outwardly influence or control another person. That pits ego against ego. It just does not work. The only thing that works is getting to the root cause of a problem and binding the spirit or demon responsible for the dysfunctional behavior of another person. Bind negative spirits by pleading the blood of Jesus Christ and by using his name. Then call on Archangel Michael to come and assist.

Sometimes there are spirits of fear or anger coming from within us. It is always good to bind any spirits around you if you are starting to feel depressed or angry. We must realize that spiritual warfare begins in our own mind. If we can assess our own minds and thoughts, we will be able to recognize and neutralize negative thoughts as they try to come in. It is important not to accept negative thoughts. Once negative emotions come in, they tend to consume us, and negative emotional states leave us vulnerable to fear. Call on the angels for help when you recognize it is happening, and worship God and ask for His help as well.

Summary of Key Points

We learned how to use spiritual warfare tools and techniques that will enable us to control and bind spirits of depression or anger before they can consume us. Now that we have prepared ourselves and understand what the tools are, I encourage you to use these techniques as needed to protect yourself from negativity in your every-day life.

* Envelop yourself in the white light of the Holy Spirit, then a layer of purple light, and then a layer of blue light for daily protection.
* Call on the authority of Jesus Christ name and plead the blood of Jesus Christ to command all spirits to go to the second dimension.
* Call on Archangel Michael and his blue flame for protection. Ask for his shields to surround you.
* Call on the Angelic Host to bring down the sacred fire of love and perfection into any situation.
* Use the violet flame of Saint Germain and Archangel Zadkiel to clear out and transmute all negativity.
* Bind spirits by speaking the word of God in the name of Jesus Christ and his authority.
* Call on your higher self for help in difficult situations.
* Use the cosmic-blue, fiery-lightning flame of the Christ against negativity.

PART II

IDENTIFYING AND RESPONDING TO DEMONS, GHOSTS, AND SPIRIT GUIDES

CHAPTER 8

UNDERSTANDING THE DIFFERENCE BETWEEN DEMONS, GHOSTS, AND SPIRIT GUIDES

Beloved, believe not every spirit, but try the spirits whether they are of God.

—I John 4:1 KJV

In the last chapter, we discovered the tools of spiritual warfare and how to use them. In this chapter, we are going to describe the differences between, spirits, demons, ghosts, and spirit guides.

The Difference Between a Spirit and a Ghost

Have you ever wondered what the differences are between a spirit and a ghost? Many people think they are the same thing, but that is not accurate. A spirit has never been born into a physical body. Most people cannot see spirits, but if you do see a spirit, you will see it out of the corner of your eye. Spirits are usually negative. They float above the ground and fly around quickly. Negative spirits or demons usually intend to distract you by bringing you negative thoughts so you will get discouraged, depressed, or angry. Demonic spirits cause confusion, disorientation, self-doubt, fear, and thoughts of suicide. I also believe that spirits can create pain in the body, because that happened to me. Demons are negative spirits that work for Satan; he directs them to affect us in destructive ways. Most demons are sent to us to tempt us to sin or to place obstacles in our path.

Ghosts are people who lived among us on earth, in human form, and who died. A ghost shuffles along the ground and appears to look human. People can also see ghosts as orbs or as spiritual beings on the other side. Usually a ghost's personality is the same as it was when he or she was alive. Many ghosts do not realize they are dead, often because they died unexpectedly or in an accident. We refer to ghosts who should move on but do not as "earthbound." They usually have unfinished business here. Ghosts may remain in our realm before moving into the light because they want to resolve problems or issues or want to be sure their loved ones will be okay. Other ghosts simply stay because they enjoy earthly pleasures—these ghosts often hang around an alcoholic or a gambler to experience his or her pleasure. When ghosts are noisy or rambunctious, it is usually because they are trying to get our attention and want to deliver a message or because they are angry that we are in their "territory" or home.

Ghosts can also be your deceased loved ones coming back to visit. You will recognize by a ghost's voice and energy that it is someone you knew.

Spirit Guides

Most people believe that angels, deceased loved ones, spirits, celestial beings, master teachers, and the Ascended Masters all fall into the category of "spirit guides." I disagree with that. In my experience, a spirit guide is usually either a deceased loved one who has come back to help guide you and protect you in your life or a loved one from a past life coming here to help you now. I believe all spirit guides were once human beings.

Before you contact any spiritual being, be sure to protect yourself and ground yourself. Always be discerning about the guidance coming through; ask for the highest guidance.

What a spirit guide should do is give you options and information that may assist you with your purpose in life. They were once human beings, so they still have the personalities that they had on Earth. The information the spirit guides present to you may not be the most reliable, but by accessing the spirit realm you give yourself access to a large number of opinions, and you can sort through those opinions for advice.

A spirit guide usually stays with you for a short while, until you learn a lesson or complete a project. Once you advance spiritually, he or she will leave, and a new spirit guide or master teacher will come in to instruct you until you learn your next lesson. Spirit guides come and go throughout your lifetime.

A spirit guide's knowledge is based on what he or she learned while on earth—they do not have a direct channel of communication with God, as the angels do. Spirit guides can be beneficial, if they can help you in a particular area, but I have learned to be very selective in whose guidance I accept. Be certain that you want guidance from a particular being before you give it permission to contact you. Remember to protect yourself and set your limits.

Spirit Attachments

What is a spirit attachment? A spirit attachment can be either a deceased loved one that has attached onto your aura or a negative spirit called a demon. The spirits attach to you for different reasons. Deceased loved ones normally attach because they want to experience a habit that they had when they were alive. They do this through you if you happen to have the same habit—drinking alcohol or smoking, for example. Most often, a negative spirit or demon will attach to your aura to drain you of energy and to feed off any negative emotions that you may have. A demon's mission is accomplished if he can prevent you from completing your purpose on earth by making you feel confused, distracted, or depressed.

How do you know if you have a spirit attachment? Negative thoughts could come into your mind, pushing you to be more aggressive or even destructive to yourself. All of a sudden, you might experience a change in your personality or pick up habits that you never had before.

Your behavior might change, and even the way you dress might change. You could have cravings for different foods that you never ate before. You could become very abusive in your relationships and even become violent at times. These are some of the symptoms of a spirit attachment. Some symptoms may not be this severe but will still be noticed by others. Often people will not realize that they have spirit attachments until the symptoms become severe and they recognize that they are doing things they never did before. Such a person will question why all of a sudden he or she has a craving for alcohol. Other people will also be curious, wondering why all of a sudden that person is drinking alcohol when it was never a habit before. Sometimes a healthy person will become constantly sick and exhausted, without knowing why. Panic attacks may develop, along with periods of extreme fear or anger.

How does one pick up spirits and demons? When the aura is unprotected and weakened by tears, cracks, and holes, spirits can attach at those points. If this is not corrected, people can take advantage of you and you will attract abusive relationships. You will also feel overwhelmed by others feelings, needs, and problems. To seal up the aura of tears, cracks, and holes, call on Archangel Michael to come with his blue light of protection and give him permission to seal up your aura after he removes the spirit attachments. It is very important to be sure to take care of your spiritual aura and boundaries, keeping them clean and fortified with Archangel Michael and Archangel Raphael's help. If someone is involved with the occult, a lot of spirit activity will surround that person; if the person is not grounded and spiritually protected, a spirit attachment can also occur. There is a spirit behind each negative emotion or traumatic experience. If we grow up in a dysfunctional family where there is abuse, rejection, depression, or criticism, we can pick up these spirits. Sin will also lead to a negative spirit attachment. When someone is practicing a sin like adultery, lying, or stealing, that person will attract these same types of spirits, to reinforce the negative behavior. You can also pick up spirit attachments by the people you hang around with through energy transference. For instance, if your friend is depressed and sad all the time, a spirit attachment could be causing these feelings, and be transferred to you. To resolve this problem do not accept the negative feelings and replace them with positive affirmations in your mind. Then call on Archangel Michael to clear your aura and protect you.

Where can a person pick up a demon or the spirit of a loved one who is deceased? These spirits can often be picked up in a hospital, bar, casino, or after an accident where the person goes into shock, and loses consciousness.

How can a person pick up a demon or the spirit of a loved one who is deceased? Activities as automatic writing and playing with the Ouija board can open up the aura and allow negative spirits, and deceased loved ones to attach onto a person. If you lived with parents that had attachments when you were a child, it is very possible that you will have a spirit attachment. If you are seeking, guidance from a spirit guide be sure to specify which particular being you want to receive guidance from. Do not ask just anybody to bring you guidance from the other side.

This is why it is very important to ground yourself and to protect yourself with the spiritual techniques I mentioned in earlier chapters. Archangel Michael will protect you if you give him permission and call on him to be with you throughout each day. If you are having any of these problems with spirit attachments, go back to the chapters on spiritual warfare within this book and apply the techniques to yourself.

Experiencing a Spirit Attachment

When I moved to Sedona, a spirit of some kind attached itself to me and created pain in my body whenever I did not do what it wanted. What the spirit wanted me to do was to fulfill my purpose in studying metaphysics and crystal healing. That does not seem like a bad thing on the surface. The way that it directed me, though, was through suffering. The voice sent into my mind was very demanding, pushy, and controlling. This was in 1992, when I was not familiar with spirits or how to release them. I knew that a spirit had attached itself to me, but I did not know what to do about it. I went to a friend, Rose, to be cleared. She helped the spirit detach from me and sent it to where it was supposed to go. I was very grateful, and I have never heard that pushy voice inside my head again. I was free.

Since then, I have learned techniques for releasing spirits. If you are hearing harassing voices in your mind, plead the blood of Jesus Christ over your mind by faith, if you are a believer. Command that the spirits go, in Jesus Christ name. The blood will silence any unwanted voices, and you will be set free. The blood of Christ overcame death and the Devil; all demons must obey the name of Jesus Christ. No weapon formed against you will prosper. You will be able to stop the devil's strategy and assignment for your life through the blood of Jesus Christ. This is activated by faith, through the authority and name of Jesus Christ, who died and was resurrected. Christ's blood can take care of all spirits of depression, poverty, fear, shame, and guilt. All feelings, memories, and thoughts that haunt you can be cleansed and cleared out by placing Christ's blood over them. *"Greater is he that is in you than he that is in the world"* (1 John 4:4 KJV).

We have the power and authority through Jesus Christ name to bind the spirits of fear and to command the works of the enemy to stop in our life. We can then begin to heal and prosper. We can speak to the situation or sickness and command it to be removed out of our life or healed by the name and blood of Jesus Christ.

It is very important to go through protection techniques and to ground your energy in the morning before you leave the house, so that an unwanted spirit will not attach to you. You have already learned how to call on the angels and give permission for the angels to help you. Disciplining your mind and reaching toward the highest truth and the light will protect you. If you find your spiritual path and follow it, putting God first, the angels will be around you to protect you.

CHAPTER 9

RESPONDING TO DIFFERENT TYPES OF SPIRITS IF CONTACTED

———◆———

Hereby know ye the spirit of God: Every
spirit that confesseth that Jesus Christ
is come in the flesh is of God.

—1 JOHN 4:2 KJV

For we wrestle not against flesh and blood,
but against principalities, against powers,
against the rulers of the darkness of this world,
against spiritual wickedness in high places.

—EPHESIANS 6:12 KJV

They were all amazed, and spake among
themselves, saying, what a word is this! For
with authority and power he commandeth
the unclean spirits, and they come out.

—LUKE 4:36 KJV

*And the seventy returned again with
joy, saying, Lord, even the devils are
subject unto us through thy name.*

—LUKE 10:17 KJV

In the last chapter, we talked about the different types of spiritual beings. These included demons, spirits, ghosts, and spirit guides. In this chapter, we will be talking about how to respond to all these different types of spirits as well as fairies, elementals, shadow people, and Master teachers.

Shadow People

What is a shadow person? If there was a shadow person around, how would you be able to recognize it? Do you know how to respond to a shadow person?

A shadow person is a spirit that appears black but transparent—hence the name. It sometimes looks like a man wearing a top hat; much like President Lincoln wore. Most often, the spirit is demonic in nature and is inter-dimensional. Fear is usually associated with it. Usually you will see a shadow person out of the corner of your eye, which might cause you to think maybe it is just your imagination. It is real! I had an experience in Sedona where I saw a shadow person in my apartment. It walked right through my bedroom and through the wall into my neighbor's apartment. It totally ignored me. At the time, I did not feel anything at all beyond shock at what I was seeing.

The next day, I saw my neighbor and asked her, "Did anything unusual happen yesterday, in the early evening?" She responded, "Yes, something unusual did happen! I saw a spirit being—black and with a hat on. It walked through your wall and into my bedroom. Then it tried to get into bed with me! My niece was visiting me, and we both jumped out of the bed. We watched it walk through our bedroom, into the living room, and then out the glass door." I told her that I had seen the shadow person, too. We had seen the same thing—it was not our imaginations. It never happened again. I often wonder whether, if I had gone to bed early that night, that shadow being would have gotten into my bed!

If you ever see a shadow person, just let it go on its way. There is no reason to try to communicate with it. You do not want to invite the negative into your life. If it does something, you do not want it to, send it to the second dimension in Jesus Christ name and authority, and plead the blood of Jesus Christ over you. Call on Archangel Michael to come and assist you. He will take it where it is supposed to go. It is best not to communicate with shadow people directly.

Energy Vampires and Spirit Attachments

Energy vampires are people who drain your energy. They have spirit attachments and entities. They are usually negative, fearful, and unhappy. They always want attention. They are big complainers who feel like victims and blame others for their problems. They make you feel guilty by embracing the "poor me" attitude. Not all energy vampires have all these traits. Some do not even know they are energy vampires. Most of them have spirit attachments taking their energy away. Drained of their own energy, they try to take energy from other people who have healthy auras.

A lot of them know that people do not want to be around them. I had customers in my workplace who came in and seemed like normal folks. I had great conversations with them, but I could feel myself getting a headache and feeling tired. They were draining my energy. Immediately I placed a copper-colored light around myself as a barrier. This light will stop any energy taken away from you. Then in your mind say, you cannot take my energy. It is as if you are making a decision by your will and visualizing that you are protected. You are not going to allow them to do it. You can call on Archangel Michael in your mind and give him permission to protect you. He will place a shield like a force field in front of you. After the people leave, have Archangel Michael cut the cords between you and those people with his golden sword of the Spirit. Give him permission to do it, and he will. Then Archangel Raphael will bring the healing. While talking to the energy vampire, send that person the pink light of unconditional love. As you do this, all negativity will be neutralized and brought into harmony. This will keep your aura strong. Another thing you can do while in the presence of an energy vampire is to use the white light and then the violet flame. Call on Saint Germain with the violet flame to come and clear out the area and transmute any negativity. Then visualize the white light once again.

Energy vampires are a problem because they are not being protected and have been attacked psychically

themselves. Their negative emotions are attracting negative spirits to them. The blue-silver light is good to visualize around energy vampires to protect and cleanse them
from negativity. Once the spirit attachments have been
removed by asking Archangel Michael, then the energy
vampires will change and stop draining other people's
energy.

Fairies

What is a fairy? A fairy is a small spirit being that has
intelligence with supernatural powers. It can also be
called a leprechaun. They live in another dimension, so
usually we cannot see them. If you are able to see them,
you will see what looks like a little body with very small to
large wings.

If a fairy contacts you, ask it what it wants and why it
has come to you. If it plays games with you and acts mischievous, you must use an authoritative voice and command it to stop bothering you. Fairies love to steal small
items; you can command them to return them. There are
good fairies and evil fairies. To attract the good ones,
go out in nature among the flowers and watch the but-
terflies. Fairies love fountains and gardens. Walk among
the trees and nature. Quiet yourself and talk gently to
the fairies. Tell them you want to work with them. Fairies
can assist you with manifesting prosperity. If you have a
good heart and good intentions, they will want to work
with you. Send out loving intentions; they can read your
thoughts and your emotions. Good fairies, usually flower
fairies and earth fairies, are friendly and want to bring
you prosperity. If you come across mischievous fairies,

command them to go back to where they came from in the name of Jesus Christ and in an authoritative voice. If they have a negative intention towards you, they can create confusion and distraction within your mind. If you do not want to be bothered by negative fairies, you can hang a cross on your door and in your car.

I had an encounter with a fairy on the way to work and at work. I did not know anything about fairies back in 2005 when this happened. One morning, I happened to put on a fairy pendant I had bought the day before. The pendant was supposed to attract fairies to you—I thought I would attract only good fairies! I was in a hurry, so I placed a large ring of mine in my purse, in a side pouch. I figured I could put it on my finger while I was at a red light. I am certain I put it in my purse—it is a very large ring, about an inch wide, and it has jade on it. When I reached down into my purse a few minutes later, there was no ring. I could not believe it. I started getting upset. It had been my grandmother's ring, and it was from the early 1900s. I looked again, but I could not find the ring. I even pulled over onto the side of the road and emptied out my entire purse—gone. Then I realized it might have been a fairy playing games with me. I started talking to the fairies. I told them in an authoritative voice that they had to return the ring. All of a sudden, the ring appeared right before my eyes—in the side pouch where I had put it originally! I was so relieved to get my ring back.

Then I continued driving to work. I was working in a retail store in a casino mall, and I was alone on shift that day. A friend of mine, Ron, worked at the kiosk in the middle of the shopping mall. He came into the store to visit me at one point. He was a young kid at the time, always joking around. At one point, he moved behind the back counter while he was talking to me. The store had a small closet where I put my lunch and my water. I went over to the closet and opened its door to get a drink of water. My food, my water, and my lunch were gone! I could not believe my eyes. I looked at Ron and told him what had happened. I knew he did not take them, because he had not been near the closet. It was a mystery to both of us. I closed the door and walked away.

I started talking to the fairies again and told them in an authoritative voice that they had to return my food and water. When I had finished, I walked over to the closet and opened the door—my food was back! Ron had seen the closet when the food was gone, and we had not gone near the closet since we discovered the food was missing. Ron was not a believer in angels, spirits, or fairies—until that day!

After that, one of the keys went missing for the merchandise cases. It was getting late, and I was about ready to close the store, but I could not leave until all the keys were accounted for and the cases were locked. At first, I thought it was Ron playing a joke on me, but he swore he had not done anything. I was getting upset. I told Ron it was a security issue and asked him to give me back the key. I told him if we did not find it, I was going to have to call the owner, and he was not going to be happy. Ron swore that he had not taken the key and said he would not joke about anything that serious. At first, I did not believe him, but then it dawned on me that the fairies were playing games with us again.

The key fit a bullet lock—the kind where you have to turn it and then pull out the bullet from the glass. We both looked on the floor, on the counters, everywhere— no key. It would have been easy to find it on the floor, since it was large. I decided to talk to the fairies and command them to bring the key back. As Ron and I were talking about the situation, I turned around. All of a sudden, the key was back in the lock! The fairies had brought it. Ron and I could not believe what had just happened. I was so relieved that the key was back in the case and that I would not have to call the owner that night. I decided I did not want to have anything more to do with fairies! I drove home, took the pendant off, and threw it in a dumpster.

Elementals

Elementals are related to the elements of water, air, fire, and earth. Elementals are considered fairies and are called different names according to the element they are associated with. The salamander is in the fire, a sylph is related to air and in the wind, an undine is related to water and is the spirit within the water, and a gnome is related to the earth. Elementals are in all things. The ones that fly usually have rounded or shaped wings like a butterfly. You can recognize an elemental or fairy by a sparkle of light appearing out of nowhere. Sometimes things will disappear and then reappear. Then you know a fairy or elemental is around.

In late June 2013, I had a health issue involving an adverse reaction to a B12 pill. It affected my nervous system, and I suffered intermittent numbness in my body after that, especially when I ate certain foods. The angels' guidance about the situation was to suggest that I cut back to three days a week at my job. I could not do that because of my financial obligations. I wanted to obey the guidance of the angels, but my bank account and ego would not allow me to do it.

They told me if I didn't cut to three days a week voluntarily, something would happen to force me to cut back my hours. I still could not bring myself to do it. One night, at about three in the morning, I awoke to see a spirit being come through my window. It was a sparkling, blue-white light in the form of a cross; it flickered and shimmered. It appeared to have a very thin body and was about three feet tall. It floated into the room and landed on my feet. I was in such shock at seeing the spirit being that I could not react. Then it floated back up and out of the room, through the same window it had come in. When it had touched my feet, I felt absolutely nothing, which was unusual because I normally would feel something and get a message. It was hot and I did not have a bed sheet over me.

To this day, I am not sure what that spirit was, but I think it might have been an elemental spirit of the air. One thing I do know is that it was karmic in nature and that it was sent to me for a reason. At first, I thought it was to heal me, but nothing changed with my numbness. The end of June came and went. On the Fourth of July, my symptoms escalated. I felt intermittent numbness throughout my body and on my face. I was at work when it happened, and I had to leave. I went to the emergency room, thinking I might be having a stroke. It turned out that everything was normal on the tests—no stroke or heart attack. I was told it was not a life-threatening situation. The doctors did not know what had caused it, but they sent me home and told me to take the next day off.

I knew at that point that this was the sign I should cut back to three days a week. I told work that I had to cut my hours until I got better. They let me do it, so I worked three days a week for about the next five to six months. Then the owner asked me to work four days a week, so I did. I promised myself at that point that if I worked four days a week I would still make time to work on this book. I did, and that schedule lasted for about three months.

I decided to teach a couple of classes on the Archangels, because I had three days off a week. I had a feeling, though, that as soon as I started teaching, the owner would ask me to work five days a week again. The day before I was going to teach my first class, I got a phone call from the owner—asking me to work five nights a week! He told me he really needed me to do it. I could not believe the timing. My intuition had been correct about the situation. I knew then that I would have to discipline myself if I was going to have time to not only prepare and teach the classes, but also to write this book. The more pressure I am under and the less time I have, the more I seem to get done, but that does not mean I enjoy such a busy schedule. I promised myself that I would work five nights a week only if I could make time to work on this book also. That is what I did. I did learn an important lesson: listen to the guidance that the angels give you, and obey. You will save yourself a lot of heartache if you do.

God's plan is not necessarily our plan, and His ways are not necessarily our ways.

The Fluorite Stone

Elemental entities can inhabit certain gemstones. One day, I went to a gem show with a friend. All of a sudden, I heard a voice in my head. At first, I thought it was an audible voice from someone nearby. It said, "Help me, help me." I walked over toward a table where I thought the voice was coming from, and I saw a large purple fluorite stone about three inches long by two inches wide. It was beautiful. I heard the voice again; it was coming from that stone, and it said, "Buy me, buy me." Therefore, I did.

I took the fluorite home, and before long, I started carrying it to work because I had noticed I felt stronger whenever I held it. I started communicating with the elemental spirit within the stone as well. My health improved, and I became stronger every day. It gave me energy and optimism.

After about six months, the elemental asked me to free it from the gemstone. I was sad about that, but I decided to do what it asked on Saint Patrick's Day. On that day, through meditation and visualization, I opened a spiritual doorway and released the elemental spirit from the stone. I saw it leave the gemstone and run into the garden area in front of where I lived. I never heard from it again. After that, it was just a rock—there was no life to it. I felt very sad and empty. It was as if I had lost my best friend. Later, I learned that elemental spirits could evolve into a higher consciousness if they perform services for others.

It had to be freed in order to evolve into a higher consciousness, so I know what I did was right.

Responding to Spirit Guides

Spirit guides once lived in a human body and now act as protectors or guides to each one of us. A person can have many spirit guides. True spirit guides are assigned to us before we are born. Other spirit guides may find us and want to communicate with us. Always discern the guidance that comes through, and then make your own choices and decisions. To respond to a spirit guide, it is best to find out who it is before you give it permission to speak to you. There are many types of spirit guides. They can hear us, direct us, and teach us. They usually guide us through our intuition. They can use synchronicities, people, nature, and events to give us a message. They continue to try to get the message across until we understand it. Spirit guides tend to point us in the direction that we need to go according to God's will and purpose for our life. Their messages can come through coins, feathers, or orbs that appear to us, or through repeated number sequences or synchronicities. Spirit guides can speak through nature, as when you see a hummingbird or butterfly where normally you would not. Even in your dreams, they can communicate to you. They like to advise us and to help us make decisions in life. Sometimes they arrange situations where we will meet a particular person or be in a situation to help us fulfill our purpose.

When you respond to spirit guides, ask a question, and they will answer you by sending thoughts into your mind. When they start communicating with you, you will be able to tell by their vibration if they are of a higher frequency or a lower frequency than you are. Take their advice with a grain of salt. Be sure to make your own decisions, and do not let anybody push you into doing something you do not want to do. The lower frequency spirit guides are very opinionated and will try to influence you into something you may not be ready for. It is important for you to realize that it is up to you to make the best decision for yourself. Ask if a spirit was born in a human body; if he or she says yes, you will know you are hearing from a spirit guide. If the answer if no, then it is probably your Guardian Angel talking to you. When you respond to spirit guides, pay attention to how you feel. Do you feel love, peace, joy, and a higher vibrational frequency, or do you feel a lower vibration that creates sadness, doubt, confusion or depression? You can ask spirit guides if they come in the light and work with Jesus Christ. If they say no, then I would not accept their guidance. Be sure to set boundaries with spirits. If you do not want to listen to them, say no. They cannot interfere with your life or give you information if you do not give them permission to do so. You are in control.

When I first started opening up to channeling, all of the spirit guides wanted to speak to me at the same time. They were lining up to talk to me. I could see them. At first, I let each speak to me in turn. Then it got to the point where there were too many, and they would start talking at the same time. I was too open. For a while, I let them channel through me until I realized that these spirit guides were once human and not necessarily any smarter than I was! After they pulled me all different directions, I decided I had enough. I told them I was not going to talk to any of them anymore.

I developed a migraine headache that lasted for about two weeks. I could not figure out why. I had forgotten that I cut off all guidance, denying permission for the spirit guides to talk to me. I had also had ringing in my ears occasionally, and that stopped as well. When you have ringing in your left ear, your spirit guides are usually downloading information and guidance. Later on, the guidance will be made known to you. All of a sudden, when you are driving or doing something else, an idea, message, or flash of insight will come to you.

I continued to have the headache. I decided I would open myself up as a channel, and ask the headache or part of the body to speak and tell me what was going on. I gave it permission, and it said, we have been knocking on your head, and you are not listening. It was my spirit guides talking to me in my mind. They said I was stubborn, so they knocked harder, causing the headache. They told me: because you are not listening, you have shut yourself off from our communication, and we do not like it. You have abandoned us. We are trying to get through to you. I told them I wanted to correct this.

The spirit guides continued: Then reconnect to our guidance. We have messages for you. We are knocking on your head. We were once human like you. You can accept or reject our information, but please at least listen to us, and do not shut us out. You are resisting events and people, not allowing joy and fun in your life. You need to do what you really want in order to be happy. Do not allow restrictions and other people to hinder you. Talk to us. Whether you take our advice or not is your decision. Do not shun us. We were sent from the other side to help you. If you do not listen to us, it can be more difficult for you. We are here to advise you on the more physical side of life. We are specialized in different areas within the physical plane to help you. We do not want you to struggle on your own. Because of some belief or fear, you are restricting yourself and limiting the many possibilities out there.

That day I realized that these spirit guides had been assigned to me on the other side before I came into this incarnation. I also realized that they have special expertise in different areas within the physical life. They give advice for our everyday activities within this material world. Angels, who are more spiritual, also told me that I was holding myself back if I cut off their guidance. I need their help to achieve my purpose in this life. They told me they had been assigned to me for this life to help me fulfill my purpose. After I understood the guidance I received, the headache disappeared within a few hours. The spirit guides who are assigned to me now have permission to bring me guidance and advice. I also realize I do not have to take their advice. I have choices.

Master Teachers

Master teachers come and go during your lifetime. They are enlightened beings that have learned their lessons and have attained a higher consciousness. While they lived on the earth plane, they mastered the elements. Now they come back to assist us in doing the same. Master teachers help you learn the lessons that you came down to earth to learn. Most likely, these lessons are being continued from a past life; it often takes us several lifetimes to learn a specific lesson. Each Master teacher will stay with you until you learn the lesson that you came here to learn. Unfinished business from a past life must often be completed in our present life.

These teachers also help us to remember what we need to accomplish in life. They are here to help us fulfill our greater purpose. Master teachers are more advanced than spirit guides are on a spiritual-consciousness level. If a master teacher contacts you, ask him or her questions about your life purpose and the lessons that you came down here to learn. Be sure to investigate and confirm whether it really is a Master teacher contacting you. Then you can give permission for the information to be given to you.

Demons and Entities

A demon is a fallen angel. Lucifer was a cherub—God's favorite angel, in fact. When he became disobedient, he was thrown out of heaven. One third of the angels followed him. Lucifer wanted to have power and be like God. Once he got to Earth, he decided that it was his territory. The demons under Satan try to distract you, bring confusion and depression, so you turn away from God.

God created man in His image and gave him dominion over all other beings. Then man sinned. God decided he would send Jesus Christ down to die for humanity's sins. Jesus Christ's resurrection overcame death and the

Devil. This restored man's relationship with God. The Devil knows man has authority over him. To access this authority, we must believe that Christ is the Son of God who died for our sins and rose from the dead. We are connected with Jesus Christ as joint heirs of Christ and heirs of God. All we have to do is to exercise our authority as Jesus did, using His name and authority and pleading the blood of Christ to command the demons to leave and go to the second dimension. We can also call on Archangel Michael to come and take the demons away to a holding place where they will be guarded by the angels until God redirects them to where they are supposed to be.

> *"And there was in their synagogue a man with an unclean spirit; and he cried out, saying, let us alone; what have we to do with thee, thou Jesus of Nazareth? Art thou come to destroy us? I know thee who thou art, the Holy One of God. And Jesus rebuked him, saying, Hold thy peace, and come out of him. And when the unclean spirit had torn him, and cried with a loud voice, he came out of him. And they were all amazed, insomuch that they questioned among themselves, saying, what thing is this? What new doctrine is this? For with authority commanded he even the unclean spirits, and they do obey him"(Mark 1:23–27 KJV).*

We have already won, through Jesus Christ's blood and the authority of his name. Christ has already defeated the Devil and overcame him with his blood. Satan will try to distract you from turning to God and fulfilling your purpose. As we use the tools of spiritual warfare, we have authority over the Devil on Earth. We must acknowledge our authority and the angels around us; that will help us through this life. The angels of the spiritual realms are waiting for us to call on them and give them permission to help us.

How Demons can Come into Your Life

Demons can enter into your life in several ways. They will be attracted to you if you have an illness or an accident. Being involved in sin, the occult, drugs, or alcohol, will attract demons. Emotional trauma and fear can bring demons into your life. Awareness is the key to discovering and sensing what is around you; it helps you watch the thoughts that come into your mind so you can cancel negative thoughts and replace them with positive thoughts. For starters, be sure to place protection around yourself every day. We can take authority over these negative spirits in Jesus Christ name.

> *"For the weapons of our warfare are not carnal, but mighty through God to the pulling down of strongholds; Casting down imaginations, and every high thing that exalted itself against the knowledge of God, and bringing into captivity every thought to the obedience of Christ;" (2 Corinthians 10:4-5 KJV).*

In Shakuntala Modi's book *Remarkable Healings,* a psychiatrist discovers unsuspected roots of mental and physical illness. She mentions that seventy-seven out of every hundred patients reported having demons that were responsible for the psychological and physical symptoms for which the patients were seeking help. "With the removal of the so-called demons, the associated symptoms caused by them were often cleared out immediately," she reports.

In William J. Baldwin's book *Spirit Releasement Therapy*, the author states, "Earthbound spirits, that is, the spirits of deceased humans, have identifiable characteristics and signs of attachment. They feel and express human emotions and can influence the human emotions by imposing their own emotional residue." I agree with this, because I myself experienced anger and depression that I picked up from a ghost in my house. Ghosts do transfer their emotions to us—and their beliefs and opinions. If a ghost continues to be around one person for a long time, a personality change can occur in that person.

How to Know if You are Being Psychically Attacked

When you are under psychic attack, you may begin to have nightmares and insomnia. You may be constantly sick and feel weak. Suicidal thoughts may come to you, along with a general feeling of hopelessness and depression. Headaches or other aches and pains may occur. You may see shadow people moving past you, out of the corner of your eye. Demons and negative spirits will transfer thoughts to you that are self-destructive, negative, and critical in order to distract you or influence you. These spirits want to destroy your self-confidence and make you depressed. Their job is to distance you from God in any way they can. They will invent distractions and problems to get you to focus on anything but God. If you remember to pray daily and remain close to God, however, you

will be able to use Christ's name and blood to send negative spirits to the second dimension. It is a battle of the
mind. As negative thoughts come, do not accept them.
Replace them with loving, positive thoughts.

A negative spirit can attach to a living person. A
particular person could also be sending you negative
thoughts. The more negative a person is, the more he or
she will attract negative spirits. It is important to place
layers of white, purple, and blue light around yourself
for protection. Negative spirits are afraid of the white
light because they believe it will kill or injure them.
The truth of the matter is that every spirit has a very
small portion of white light within, since everything
originated with God. Satan does not want these negative spirits to have this information. This white light can
be expanded and will overcome the darkness; the spirits can raise their consciousness if they choose to. Most
negative spirits do not choose to follow the light. They
are afraid of it. It is true that white light will fracture
these beings if they are exposed to it.

To respond to a demon or negative spirit, you can
command it to go to the second dimension in Jesus
Christ name and authority and by his blood. Then you
can call on Archangel Michael to come and assist you further; remember to give him permission to take the spirits to a holding place where they can be guarded by the
angels until God decides where to direct them. If they
are in your house, for example, you can command them
to leave and go to the second dimension. If they do not
go, you can convince them by telling them that you will
bring the white light over them and fracture them. They

will definitely go at that point. Once they are gone, you will know and feel that your home is cleared. Be sure to bring the white light into your home. Then call on Saint Germain and his violet flame to clear the rest of your home of all negativity. Once that is done, visualize the blue light of Archangel Michael and the blue-white lightning flame of Jesus Christ going through your home. Your home will now be cleared and protected.

To prevent any further infestations of negative spirits, wash down your walls with white vinegar and water mixed together. Burn or spray sage throughout your home. Remove any articles or items that have anything to do with the occult. Start reading the Bible, which is a two-edged sword, supernatural and powerful. Then speak it aloud. Praying and worshipping God makes the negative spirits want to avoid you. It all comes down to frequency and vibration. As you pray, worship God, and read the Bible, your vibration will rise to the level of beings that function at a higher consciousness. All negative entities and spirits at a lower vibrational level will drop away. You will not be on the same frequency as they are, so you will not attract them into your life. As you change your thinking patterns to positive and loving thoughts, you will attract the angels around you.

Bible Scriptures to Help You Become Aware of God's Power and the Power of Jesus Christ Name

And these signs shall follow them that believe; in my name shall they cast out devils (Mark 16:17 KJV).

And he said unto them, I beheld Satan as lightning fall from heaven. Behold, I give unto you power to tread on serpents and scorpions, and over all the power of the enemy: and nothing shall by any means hurt you (Luke 10:18–19 KJV).

For this purpose the Son of God was manifested, that he might destroy the works of the devil (1 John 3:8 KJV).
How God anointed Jesus of Nazareth with the Holy Ghost and with power: who went about doing good, and healing all that were oppressed by the devil; for God was with Him (Acts 10:38 KJV).

Entities

Entities are negative and from another dimension. They can appear as different creatures within the spiritual realms. They are not demons or ghosts. I have found them in the spiritual realm; they want to feed off your negative emotions and your energy field. Entities may follow you around or jump from one person to another. Sensitive people are more prone to picking them up. These beings want to attach to you so they can drain your energy and control you. They can interfere with your health and happiness. Entities can cause strong addictions, depression, and confusion. They are like parasites or leeches. By feeding off your energy, they get stronger. Most entities are normally not seen; some entities can shape-shift into a physical form, but this is rare. You may simply sense when an entity is around. The same technique that you use to send demons and negative spirits also work to release entities from your presence, but you can also ask Archangel Michael to come with his golden sword of the Spirit and cut the cords between the entity and you.

Encounters with Entities

The Jumping Entity
After shopping at a store one day, I got into my car and started driving to work. I sensed that there was something in the car with me—an entity of some kind. I told it I would deal with it when I got to work. I drove into the parking lot at the casino where I was working, got out of the car, and let the entity out as well. It followed me. I talked to it a little to find out what it wanted. I was just about to send it away in Jesus's name when I saw it jump onto a woman who was gambling on a slot machine. I had to get to work, so I kept walking. Because I can deal with entities from a distance, I was able to send this entity back where it had come from.

The Spirit that Made Itself Known
One day back in 2007, I was at work selling ancient coin jewelry and artifacts in a store. A customer walked in, a man who immediately seemed a little strange. As he walked toward a large, heavy glass case to look at the jewelry, I saw that he had a spirit attachment. As I started walking toward him, the spirit attachment jumped off the man and onto the glass case. It exploded and shattered. The noise was so loud it shook me up. Small pieces of glass went everywhere, and the jewelry was exposed. The man ran out of the store quickly, leaving the mess behind.

I could not believe what had just happened. Nobody had touched that case. The glass was thick and heavy. Somehow, the spirit's negative energy had caused the case to explode. There was no earthquake or other rumbling movement in the building. I immediately spoke to the spirit and commanded it to go in Jesus Christ name.

I had received a communication from the spirit as soon as I noticed it, telling me it wanted to release itself from the man, and it needed a sound to break the connection. That seemed contrary to what I knew about spirits. Usually they want to stay with a live person and can freely move from one person to another. However, in this instance, somehow, the spirit could not get free. The man had bound it to him; he must have placed it under some kind of spell to make it do his bidding. I called the owner of the store to tell him what had happened, and then I simply took a broom and started cleaning up the glass. That was one of the strangest experiences I have ever had with a spirit, because it affected a physical object with such intense power.

A Stubborn Entity

A friend of mine moved to California and bought a house. She did not realize that many entities and spirits haunted it. A lot of occult activity had happened around the area, and although she had some experience with spiritual warfare, she did not know how to handle it. The negativity was too overwhelming. She asked for my help.

As soon as I tuned into the driveway, I sensed that there were legions of demons and entities residing in the house. I called on the Archangels and Jesus Christ name and commanded them to go to the second dimension.

They all obeyed and left over the next twenty-four hours—except for one, a stubborn entity that sat on her kitchen counter and refused to budge. He was very big and fat. I figured he would leave before long.

I talked to my girlfriend a couple days later and asked her how things were going. She told me that all the entities had left, except for a big one sitting on the kitchen counter. I had not told her about that entity! She could sense, see, and feel it in her home. I continued to work on the entity with spiritual warfare techniques. He finally left—after three days!

The Demon Visitation and Entity

One day a woman came into the store whom I had never seen before. She said she had a message for me from the Pleiadians. I asked her what it was, and she said I needed to go to Arizona to find gold. The Pleiadians needed my car to drive there, but they would show us where the gold was. I told her to come back the next day and I would bring a map, so she could show me where to go. She told me that she was visiting from Illinois, and her name was Eden. She was carrying a couple of large bags. She asked me to hold onto a pair of gloves and a bag of candy for her. I asked her why, but she said she just did not want to carry them around. Then she left, and I took the gloves and the candy away with me in a bag.

I got in my car and started driving home. I looked beside me a few minutes later, and I saw an entity in a spirit form that looked kind of like an octopus. It had long tentacles, but it was definitely not from this planet or dimension. I knew it was evil. I realized then that the entity was attached to the gloves Eden had given me. I was sitting at a stoplight, waiting to get on the freeway, when I realized all this. I immediately rolled down the window and commanded the entity to leave in Jesus Christ name and never to return. At that point, I felt the entity stumble over me to get out the open window. As it crossed my body, it left sand all over me. I could not believe what I saw. There was real sand on my legs and my arm. This is an example of an entity in a spiritual form shape shifting briefly into a physical form. I did not mention the incident to anyone.

The next day at work, Eden came back. I did not say anything to her about what had happened, but I did ask her more questions about herself. She told me she had lit a candle the night before. She had given up her will and fallen asleep. When she woke up, something was inside her, controlling her legs and arms and telling her what to do. She had no control over her own body. I could not believe what she was telling me—I did not know that was possible. Nevertheless, why would she give up her will?

Eden told me she wanted help from other dimensional beings but did not specify which ones. She should have surrendered only to God and His will. Instead, she enabled the spirits and demons to enter her and control her. The spirits told her to buy a one-way ticket to Las Vegas and to bring luggage. Then they sent her to me. It turned out that she had no place to stay and very little money, and to be honest, she rather looked like a street person to me. I knew then that this message could not have been from the Pleiadians. These were negative spirits and demons within her. I brought out the gloves and the bag of candy. She told me that I should keep them. I told her in a very firm voice, "I am giving you a choice. You will take these items back, or I will throw them away. What have you decided?" She said she would take them back.

I had brought a map of Arizona, as promised. I got it out and placed it in front of her. I said, "I want you to mark where the gold is."

She marked an X in about four different places, all unfamiliar to me. She kept insisting that I take her to Arizona so we could find the gold together. Of course, I thought that was ridiculous. Nevertheless, I did ask her more questions. I wanted to know about the spirits within her. I asked them who they were.

They said we are legion. I knew what that meant: demons. There were many. They had taken over her body. She was possessed. Her personality was buried within her. I had never come across a situation like this. I decided to keep asking questions, although I knew I was playing with fire. My mind became confused, and I almost could not do my job. Customers kept coming in; I felt totally disoriented. I realized that I was in over my head. The demons were too many and too powerful for me to handle. Eden eventually left, and then I pleaded the blood of Jesus Christ over myself and commanded all confusion and disorientation to leave in the name of Jesus Christ. Then I said a mantra for added protection. I knew I could not let her come back into the store again— it was too dangerous for me.

The next day, I saw her walk by the store, but she did not come in. A few minutes later, though, she returned and entered. She said, "I don't know why I just passed the store. I know where it is."

I told her that she had gone past the store because I did not want her there anymore. She sat down on a chair anyway and kept talking to me. I told her I was not interested in going to Arizona or giving her my car. "I am not going to go along with your plans," I said as she got up. I told her in the name of Jesus Christ to leave and never come back.

As soon as I said that, she bent over and said in a very soft voice, "Okay, okay, okay." She slowly walked out of the store, hunched over like a defeated foe. I never saw her again.

I learned from this experience that if I meet a demon or negative spirit, I need to send it away immediately and not try to engage it in conversation. It is too dangerous to communicate with demons. A ghost or the spirit of your deceased loved one is different—you will be okay. However, a demon or negative spirit simply creates confusion, disorientation, or pain in your body. Its aim is to be very destructive to you. When you respond to negative spirits and demons, it is best to use the name of Jesus Christ and his authority to send them away. Since Jesus Christ overcame death and the Devil through his blood, pleading the blood is the ultimate weapon against the Devil or any demon or negative spirit. In this situation, I saw the power of Jesus Christ name. He does have authority over a legion of demons.

Have you ever had an experience with a demon or negative spirit? How did you respond to that spirit? Now that you know this information, how would you respond differently?

Summary of Key Points

We have discussed and defined negative spirits, shadow people, demons, entities, fairies, elementals, spirit guides, and Master teachers and how to respond to them. Here are the key points to remember in engaging with each:

Demons: Command them to go in the name of Jesus Christ and by the blood of Christ and his authority. Call on Archangel Michael to come and assist if necessary to take them where they are supposed to go. Do not communicate with demons. After you command the demon to go, say, "I will send the white light to fracture you if you do not go now, in Jesus Christ name." The demon will obey Christ's authority and leave. You can also send it to the second dimension in Jesus Christ name and by his authority.

Elementals: You can respond to an elemental's presence by talking to it. Do not be surprised if there is no return communication, though. Use an authoritative voice and command it to leave.

Entities/Biological Entities: Once you find out what it is, command it to go back to where it came from, in Jesus Christ name and authority. You can communicate briefly with an entity to determine and identify that it is indeed an entity and not some other type of spirit. Be sure you put your protection on first—white light surrounded by a purple light. Call on Saint Germain and Archangel Michael to come and assist if necessary.

Fairies: You can communicate with a fairy. If you meet a mischievous one, you can choose not to play its game—just tell it to go away and not bother you anymore, or to return whatever it might have taken from you. Most likely, it will leave. You do have to use an authoritative voice when you give the command.

Master Teachers: You can listen to their guidance and then determine whether you want to follow it or not. You will be able to determine the motive of a master teacher and feel its vibration. If you feel love, you know that the master teacher is giving you guidance that is in your best interest.

Negative Spirits: It is best not to communicate with these at all. Call on Archangel Michael to come and assist you, and command them to go away in Jesus Christ name and authority. They will be sent to a holding place until God redirects them to where they are supposed to be. Visualize a white light around yourself, overlaid with a purple light, for protection.

Shadow People: Command them in the name of Jesus Christ to go away to the second dimension. Call on Archangel Michael to come and assist if necessary. Do not communicate with them.

Spirit Guides: You can communicate with a spirit guide as if it is a person. Find out its motives and intentions and why it has chosen to communicate with you. Once it gives you guidance, you can reject or accept it. You have to make your own decisions in life; remember that you have choices and free will. Spirit guides can only reveal as much knowledge as they acquired during their own lifetime; their guidance does not come from a direct link to God.

CHAPTER 10

RESPONDING TO GHOSTS

———

In the last chapter, we talked about how to respond to negative spirits, shadow people, demons, entities, fairies, elementals, spirit guides, and Master teachers. In this chapter, we will be talking about what a ghost is and how to respond to one.

All About Ghosts

Are you certain you know what a ghost really is? A ghost is a human being who has died, but who has not gone into the light. A ghost is essentially an earthbound spirit. There are several reasons why people do not go directly into the light after they die. First, they often do not realize they are dead. When some people die, they do not look up, but continue looking "down." These people continue their daily routines, the same as when they were living. Second, they may stay on Earth because of unfinished business that they feel they have to complete. For example, they want to be sure that loved ones that they left behind will be okay. They stay around because they want to give a message to a loved one. Third, some ghosts are afraid of the light or are afraid that they may go to Hell—they would rather stay on Earth than take that chance. Fourth, some have questions they want to answer before moving on. Fifth, some are looking for something or are lost and confused. Sixth, a ghost may be angry about something and become noisy and destructive and can actually break things or move things around in your house. These ghosts are trying to get your attention. They may be angry that you are in their former home or in their "territory," and they want you out. They also do not realize that they have died, which is why they see you as an intruder and are trying to scare you off. Seventh, many ghosts have demonic influence which have prevented them from going into the light and kept them earthbound. Eighth, they do not know what to do or where to go. If they do see the light, they do not know they are supposed to go into it. Ninth, they stay because they want to experience pleasure, by reliving their addictions of drinking, smoking, or gambling by attaching on to the living. To resolve these problems, you must first communicate with the ghosts to ensure that they know they are dead. First, release the demons in the name of Jesus Christ, sending them to the second dimension. Then send the ghosts into the light. I will describe the process of sending the ghosts into the light near the end of this chapter.

Before communicating with a ghost, be sure to place the white light of protection around yourself. Be sure you are feeling detached and without fear. You must talk as if you are talking to a regular person. Ask who the ghost is and what he or she wants. Is the ghost looking or waiting for something? The ghost will respond by speaking into your mind. Explain to the ghost he or she is dead and that you can send him or her into the light. Life is finished here; it is time to return to God. Ask if the ghost is ready to go into the light. If the answer is no, ask why. Most often, the ghost feels bound to stay because of unfinished business on Earth. Some ghosts do not accept that they are dead. Sometimes they will even argue with you.

Do not be alarmed if you start feeling angry or depressed while you are communicating with a ghost. Many times, ghosts are angry or depressed, and you will pick that up within yourself. To resolve how you feel, you need to send the ghost into the light and realize why those feelings are happening. It is okay to have a conversation with the ghost to determine what he or she wants done before becoming willing to move into the light. Often the ghost will be disoriented or confused. This sometimes happens when there was an unexpected death or an accident. Explain to the ghost that it is time to go into the light and be at peace. Tell him that God is love and that He will grant forgiveness to anyone who reaches out to Him. Assure the ghost that his or her loved ones have forgiven any hurts. The ghost's deceased relatives and loved ones are waiting to accompany him or her into the light. If the ghost still feels unworthy or does not want to go into the light, you must convince him or her to confess all sins and be forgiven.

Have you come across any hot or cold spots in your home, any noises you cannot explain? Do you believe you may have a ghost in your home? Do your pets look up and clearly see something that you cannot? Do you hear knocking, pounding, or banging in your home?

The Ghost Walking Through my Home

I was living in Las Vegas and renting a small house. One day as I was sitting on my bed, a ghost walked through my bedroom and right through the wall to the outside. It was a man wearing a red plaid shirt and a pair of jeans. He was probably in his forties. I saw him walk right past me. He did not talk to me or even acknowledge that I was there. He was a spirit form in another dimension. I thought it was strange that he did not see me or communicate with me. He just kept walking and continued in a straight line. I did not think about sending him into the light—it happened so fast. I never saw him again.

Ghosts sometimes try to get our attention by making noise or making things disappear from our home. Other times, they actively want to scare us. Do not be afraid when you talk to them, though—be detached. Talk to the ghost as you would to a regular person. Ask questions; tell him you are not afraid of him, and there is nothing he can do to make you afraid. When ghosts realize they cannot scare you, then they will stop trying and go away.

Carol's Experience with a Ghost

A friend of mine, Carol, was housesitting for another friend. She knew that there was a presence there because her friend had told her there was a ghost in the house. She had told them not to worry; she would deal with it. She was washing dishes when all of a sudden a presence came near her. She described it as a dark presence. She knew that it was a ghost, so she told the ghost she was not afraid. After that, the ghost disappeared. When her friend came back and asked about the ghost, Carol said, "I told it I was not afraid and that there was nothing it could do to make me upset, so I guess it left." Just talk to the ghost and ask what message it has for you. The important thing is to protect yourself and ground yourself before you start talking to any ghost.

The Deceased Children Who Appeared in my Home

I worked at a preschool back in the 1980s. I had been working there about four months when I came home one day to find a group of preschool children in my apartment—in spiritual bodies. They wanted to communicate with me. They knew they were dead and had come to me for help. There were ten children in all. They told me they had died in a fire. They wanted me to send them into the light, so I did as they asked. These steps are explained later in this chapter. The next day when I went to work, they told me that they needed to make cuts and I was going to be laid off.

The Seniors Who Appeared in my Home

After I was laid off from the preschool, I found a job as a caregiver at a home for seniors. I had been working there for a few months when I came home to my apartment one day and found deceased seniors waiting for me—just like the children I had seen before. The seniors were also ghosts who wanted to be sent into the light. They came to me for help because they did not know how to get there. Again, I did as they asked. I went to work the next day and they told me they were cutting back and had to lay me off. I then realized what was happening. I was being sent to places where ghosts needed me. I told God that I was happy to be able to help, but that it could not keep happening because I could not keep changing jobs. After that, it stopped.

Who was John King?

I moved into an apartment in Las Vegas only to find that the energy in the bedroom was very negative—I could not sleep in there. I slept in the living room for a few nights until I realized what was bothering me. There was a ghost in the bedroom. I put off dealing with the ghost, because I was very busy working at the time. Finally, I thought I really have to do something about this. I went into the room and started to meditate. I heard a male voice speaking directly into my mind. He told me his name was John King. I had been correct—he was indeed a ghost. He had lived in this apartment and died there. He said, "This is my room."

I asked what had happened to him and told him he needed to go into the light. He replied, "What do you mean? I'm not dead." I had visions of him being very ill and dying right there, in that apartment. I could see that he had been there ever since. I convinced John that he was dead and could move into the light. Then I asked the angels and his deceased relatives to come and assist him. With Archangel Azrael's assistance, he went.

Ghosts Lining Up

I once lived in a haunted house, and I had sent the ghosts into the light. It made me feel good to be helpful in that way, so I decided to send out a message in the neighborhood to all ghosts who wanted to be sent into the light. I told them they could come to me and I would help them. I figured a few ghosts would answer my call, but then I saw dozens lining up. I could not believe my eyes. I had promised to help them, so I sent every single one into the light. There were 250 ghosts by the time I had finished, from the neighborhoods all around where I lived. It took me about five hours to complete the process. I had no idea there would be that many earthbound souls around. I told myself I would never do that again!

Living in a Haunted House

One day I asked a neighbor if he had a particular tool that I could borrow. When he brought it over, he asked me, "Do you know anybody who wants to rent a house?"

"I may be interested. Tell me more," I said. Once he gave me the address, I drove down to see it. I could not believe my eyes! I had seen the exact same house in a dream the year before. I recognized it because of the salt cedar trees around it. It was exactly as the dream had portrayed it. I remember looking up to God and asking, "Do you really want me to live here?" However, I already knew the answer was yes.

After I confirmed that I wanted to move in, my neighbor told me that four ghosts, one of whom was a woman in a white gown that walked around the place, haunted the house. I told him that was not a problem, because I could clear out the ghosts. I turned out to be the perfect renter!

The Black Limo

Right after I moved into the house with the salt cedar trees, I noticed a black limo parked outside. It had been there for about an hour, so I began to wonder what its driver was doing. I figured the driver had to be watching my house. The house next door was empty, and there was no house at all on the other side—just an electrical transformer. I decided to go ask the driver what he was doing. As I walked up to the limo, I noticed a sign on the back window: Paranormal Investigations. "Hi, how are you?" I asked. "What's going on? I live over there." He seemed to be a nice person. "I'm watching the house," he said. "Why? I just moved in. Is there something I should know?" I asked. He looked past me. "There goes another one!" "Another what?" He answered, "One spirit just came out of your window and another went inside. There is all this paranormal activity in your house. Spirits and ghosts like it because it is near an electrical transformer. They are attracted to the electromagnetic field. This neighborhood is a historical landmark. Your house was built in the 1920s. We come over here on a regular basis to see the ghosts and the spirits."

I told him I was planning to clear out the ghosts and the spirits. He said, "You don't understand—the whole neighborhood is full of them." I said, "Not a problem. I can clear it."

I went back into my new house and continued to clear out the ghosts and spirits, one by one. I started with the spirits. I wiped down the walls and floors with white vinegar and water and visualized the white light and the violet flame of protection filling the house. I used sage to clear out all negativity, and then I said prayers and placed salt in the corners of the house. I sent the spirits to the second dimension in Jesus Christ name and authority and pleaded the blood of Jesus Christ. It worked. The spirits were instantly gone. Then I started to deal with the ghosts. Often, spirits are attached to ghosts and need to be released and taken away by Archangel Michael or sent to the second dimension before they can be sent into the light. I found four ghosts left in the house after the evil spirits were gone, just as my previous neighbor had told me.

I sensed and had a knowing that these ghosts were in my house. Each had a different reason for being there. One was a suicide who felt guilty for what he had done. His name was Michael. He felt he could not go into the light because of his actions. I explained to him that he was dead and that he could still confess his sin to Jesus Christ and be forgiven. After he did, he felt that he deserved to go into the light.

The other ghosts would make noises to get my attention, and there were cold spots in the bathroom. I would get chills whenever I went in there. One ghost started speaking into my mind when I went into the bathroom. She told me her name was Lucy. She had been kidnapped, bound, and murdered. Her murderer had since died too, but he kept her chained on a spiritual level by his possessiveness. She wanted to be released into the light. She told me he had killed her in 1957 and then continued to live in the house to guard her body. She asked me to go into my front yard and dig up a creature near the tree because somehow it was holding her there. I thought, "Sure, I have nothing better to do than go dig a ditch in my front yard."

Nevertheless, I did it, and I did find a creature that had been buried there. I could not identify what it might have been, and I threw it away. I went back into the house—she was gone.

The murderer died in 1968. They both stayed in the bathroom of the house after they died. He was in love with her but was jealous and possessive of her. He had murdered her because he was angry that she went out with other men. He could not have her to himself, so he chained her up and killed her. Once I sent her into the light, he came to the forefront of the ghosts in the house and began expressing his anger and depression. I communicated with him, but he did not want to go into the light. He said he could not go: he had killed a woman and she would never forgive him. I told him that she already had. I worked to convince him that if he wanted to be with her in love and forgiveness, he would have to go into the light too. He finally agreed to confess his sin and go up into the light. He saw that this was the way to be with her forever.

The fourth ghost was a beautiful woman in a white gown, just as my neighbor said. She told me she had been my sister in a past life, in 1909! She wanted to watch over me and would not go into the light until her purpose was fulfilled. She told me that during a past life, we had been pioneers who came out to the West in wagons. I had died when I was about thirty-two years old, without fulfilling my life's purpose. She was there to be sure that I was not going to die early this time. She said she would stay in the house to watch over me and protect me. Once I moved away, she went into the light. She was only meant to protect me as long as I lived in that house. The house was connected energetically to another house identical in Arizona, which was a military outpost back in the late 1800's. I had gone to Arizona on a vacation and discovered an identical house like the one I lived in. It was in the middle of nowhere with only the foundation and a few walls left. There was a date and it said 1867. In the middle of nowhere, a tour guide took me there after we dug for gold. He said he wanted to show me something and did not know anything about the house that I was living in at the time. He was a complete stranger to me and a tour guide for people who wanted to go out and dig for gold. This house had large salt cedar trees around it like the house that I was living in. These large trees are not native to Arizona or Nevada and were brought to these areas and planted. The house that I lived in was a prosperity house. Once I received the prosperity, I moved. It was then that my sister from a past life knew that I would be okay and she could go into the light. She had fulfilled her purpose.

My Lost Cat Came Back

I had a black cat that would go outside but came back home every night. When he did not come back for a few days, I began to worry about him. A neighbor told me that the property owner had gathered up all the cats in the neighborhood and taken them to the pound. I was very upset, and I raced to the pound. Unfortunately, it was too late.

A few days went by. I was sitting out by the swimming pool when a cat that I did not know came running up to me. He jumped on my lap as though he knew me and sat there, purring and meowing as though he was talking to me. I really believe that it was my cat who had died, coming back to say good-bye. This cat had the same mannerisms and behavior as my cat. I believe that somehow my cat had temporarily possessed the other cat. I felt so much love, I am sure it must have been him.

Before Entering A Haunted House

What do you need to do before entering a haunted house? What should you expect once you are in a haunted house? What should you do when you come out of a haunted house, so spirits and ghosts do not follow you home?

It is very important to protect yourself before you go into a haunted house and find yourself exposed to spirits and ghosts. Visualize a white light bubble around you—this protects you on a physical level. Then visualize a purple light over the white light—this protects you on a spiritual level. Last, visualize the blue light of Archangel Michael's protection over the purple light. Call on Archangel Michael and give him permission to be with you when you walk into a haunted house. I know it is exciting to step into a haunted house; you want to be scared and feel sensations like hot spots, cold spots, to hear strange noises, or see a spirit or ghost. Have fun, but be safe. When you are ready to leave, you need to clean your aura. Have Archangel Michael cut you free and remove any attachments to spirits or ghosts. Give him permission to do this. This will prevent any spirits or ghosts from going home with you.

If you accidentally allow a spirit or ghost to go home with you, you will know it, because you will begin to have all kinds of problems and negativity in your life. It is very important to clean out your aura on a daily basis and to protect yourself every day. Grounding is also important. This will stabilize your energy field and protect you from negativity. If you do end up bringing something unwanted home, you can command it to go in the name of Jesus Christ and by his authority and blood to the second dimension. Then God will redirect it to where it should go.

If you encounter a ghost, communicate with it and ask why it is there. There are a few reasons why a ghost will hang around. Sometimes it has unfinished business or does not know it is dead. You can choose to send the ghost into the light, if it is ready to go.

Here are the steps to send a ghost into the light:

* Convince the ghost that he is dead.
* Ask if he wants to go into the light.
* Call on his dead relatives, Archangel Michael, and Archangel Azrael to come and take him into the light.
* Ask him how he wants to go up, whether in a train, a car, on a horse, or in a boat. Watch him get into the vehicle and for the angels and his deceased relatives or loved ones to escort him.
* You will know that he has reached the light when you cease to be able to communicate with him. You will feel at peace knowing he has arrived where he is supposed to be.

Ghosts communicate with us in several ways: telepathy, automatic writing, dreams, scents, hot spots, cold chills, and noises. Ghosts seem to come out more at night, perhaps because it is quieter on a psychic level when most people are sleeping. Sometimes residual hauntings result from events so traumatic they cause memories and thought forms to repeat. Spirit guides are ghosts that come back to watch over us and to guide us. They keep their personalities, as if they were still alive. Ghosts look like human beings and are dressed in clothing even in the spiritual realms. They can attach onto a person, especially if they have something in common like drinking or gambling.

Have you ever communicated with a ghost? Do you have a ghost in your house? Think back in your past, and remember if you ever had any experiences with a ghost or your deceased loved one who has died. Have you ever had your pet come back to visit you?

Summary of Key Points

Protect yourself with the white light bubble, with the purple light over that, and then the blue light, before communicating with a ghost.

- Ask the ghost why he is still on Earth.
- Convince the ghost that he is dead and that it is time for him to go into the light and be at peace. Tell him God is all loving and forgiving.
- Call the ghost's dead relatives to come and get him. Then call on the angels of the light and Archangel Azrael to come and assist.
- Explain to the ghost how to go into the light. Tell him to look up so he can see it, not down at the Earth. Tell him to greet his deceased loved ones and to go into the tunnel if one appears.
- Ask the ghost what method of transportation he wants to use to go up in.
- Visualize the ghost getting into the vehicle and going up into the light.

The ghost will be greeted by a light being who will assist him and take him where he needs to go. The ghost will go to the level where his consciousness is. Once he has gone into the light, you will sense it and not be able to communicate with him any longer.

CHAPTER 11

RESPONDING TO YOUR DECEASED LOVED ONES IF CONTACTED

———

Spirits are around us more often than not.
Some people can sense them; others can
hear them, and still more can see them.

—ANGELA THOMAS, PSYCHIC-CLAIRVOYANT

I am come a light into the world,
that whosoever believeth on me
should not abide in darkness.

—JOHN 12:46 KJV

In the last chapter, we covered how ghosts communicate with us and how we should respond to them. We also talked about the basic steps for how to send a ghost into the light. In this chapter, we will be discussing how to communicate with our deceased loved ones and how they might try to communicate with us.

Our Deceased Loved Ones Contact Us

How do your deceased loved ones communicate with you and appear to you? How do you know if a deceased loved one is trying to contact you? Even though they are dead, people we knew and loved are still alive in consciousness on the other side—they are just in a spiritual body now. Most of the time, our deceased loved ones come to us to let us know they are okay and at peace.

Usually, a loved one will send signs of their presence— a scent of cologne, or maybe cigars or cigarettes if he or she was a smoker. Spirits and ghosts love smells, so think about any scent that you associate with your deceased loved one. I had an experience recently where I walked over near my door and smelled beautiful roses—but there were none there. I do not have any rose perfume or flowers in my house. The scent lasted for a few minutes, and then disappeared. I associate roses with my father because of the roses at my father's funeral. I had placed one rose without water on the dresser after my father's funeral, and the rose stayed fresh for about two weeks.

Often, your deceased loved ones will come to you in your dreams and give you messages. If you see them in your dreams, know that it means they are watching over you and sending you love. If you do not understand the dream, it will repeat itself in different ways until you get the message. My uncle appeared in my dreams for months. I did not even know he had died, so I did not realize he was coming to me with a message.

If an animal or bird is associated with a deceased loved one who is trying to contact you, you will start seeing that animal or bird all the time. Just know that it is a reminder that your deceased loved one is around you and watching over you.

Other times, your loved ones may speak directly into your mind and give you messages. You may get flashes of insight or ideas that are new to you. Thoughts will come to you that you would not have had on your own. You will hear the voice of your loved one speaking to you in your mind. The personality of your deceased loved one will come through. Do not be afraid. Your deceased loved one is just trying to communicate with you. Talk to your loved one like he or she is still alive.

Sometimes the deceased will move objects in your home, trying to get your attention. They can turn lights on and off, for example. On the other hand, say you are having coffee in the morning, and you have a habit of always leaving your coffee cup in the same place. You may find that it has been moved to another location. A ghost is in your house! It is probably a deceased loved one trying to get your attention.

Sometimes you will see orbs that are gray-white in color floating in the air around you. Most of the time, these orbs are your deceased loved one's consciousness in spirit form. A friend of mine saw a white orb emerge from his mother's forehead after she died—he believes it was her consciousness, or soul. He described it as a spiritual sphere the size of a golf ball. Usually in a deceased orb, a face can be seen within the sphere.

Celestial beings of higher vibrations often appear as golden-colored orbs, or have specific colors associated with them. Archangel Michael, for example, can make his presence known by a blue orb or a sparkling blue light.

If you want to know whether a deceased loved one is okay and at peace, ask him or her to come to you in a dream. If the deceased loved one is earthbound and does not want to go into the light, tell him or her that death is connected to love, forgiveness, and the light of God.

Visit from Heaven

I had a dream about my cat Shawnee after he died. He was sitting on the bed, but he looked smaller and younger than he had been before death. I got so excited I went to him and hugged him. He felt like a real, physical cat. My other cat, Tiger came up on the bed. The two of them rubbed against each other. Then they kissed each other on the mouth. I hugged both of them, and was very happy. Shawnee was Tiger's brother, and he died in March 2012. They had never been separated a day of their lives. This dream was so real, I am sure it was a visit from my deceased cat.

A Twenty-Year-Old Cat, Young Again

I had a cat that lived to be twenty years old. He went blind, could not hear, and would howl and become fearful and violent. He began attacking my other cats and me. He seemed to be in pain. I decided to put him down; I loved him, but I did not have a choice. Afterward, I felt very sad and guilty. As I sat in front of the veterinarian's office in my car, I cried and cried. I was so upset I could not drive. All of a sudden, I heard a voice come into my mind and saw a vision—with my eyes open. The voice said, "I am free. I am young again! I am young again!" I saw my cat running through a field of flowers, happy as could be. I felt better then, and realized I had released him from all the suffering he had been going through here on Earth.

Responding to Your Deceased Loved One

How should you respond to a deceased loved one if contacted? First, you will want to determine if it really is your deceased loved one. Be sure to ask the ghost's name. Ask about something he or she did in waking life on Earth. Ask about a situation only the two of you knew about. You should recognize the voice and personality, the way the ghost speaks to you. For example, my stepdad would have to open the hood of his Cadillac and pour gasoline on the engine to make it go. My mom and I were the only ones who knew about this. There was also the time when he told me he loved me when we were standing by the barbecue. He died a week later. Either of those types of details would be perfect for confirming a ghost's identity.

Once you determine it is your deceased loved one, then you can begin to ask questions. He or she will send messages or talk directly into your mind. You will feel a loving presence around you, and this lets you know he or she is happy and at peace. It is common for a deceased loved one to come to you in a dream. Sometimes a ghost will appear to you as a spiritual being in the middle of the night to try to give you a message as well. Do not be afraid—just ask questions until you recognize who it is.

Talk to the deceased as if you would talk to your grandmother. You can also ask for help.

Once your deceased loved ones cross over into the light, they will be in a loving and forgiving environment. In the process of crossing over to the other side, they will always have a guide. If they choose not to go into the light, but stay in darkness by their own free will, they will either stay earthbound or go to a holding area until they can be directed to another place.

My Dying Mother's Conversation

I was at my mother's bedside while she was dying. She was glowing and smiling as she explained how she was seeing her dead relatives, Jesus, and the angels. After she died, I heard her voice in my room. She was calling to me. She told me she was okay, young, and happy again. (David)

I Am Not Dead!

One day, I woke up and heard rattling in the kitchen. I got up and went to investigate. I saw my dishes shaking in the dish rack on the counter. I thought it must be a spirit or my Guardian Angel. This went on for a couple of weeks. My stepdad had died about two weeks earlier. I decided I would go into meditation, see if I could communicate with him, and learn whether he was trying to communicate with me.

About a year before, I had taken a workshop on how to communicate and send deceased loved ones into the light. I began meditating, found my stepdad, and proceeded to communicate with him by asking questions.

Sure enough, he said he was rattling the dishes to get my attention. I told him he was dead. He told me he was not dead—and he was very stubborn about it. It took me forty-five minutes to convince him that he was. I knew who he was through his voice and his personality. I talked to him as if he was a person, explained how and why he should be sent up into the light, and then asked him if he wanted to go. After he decided he was ready, I asked him how he wanted to go up. He said, "In my Cadillac, of course!" I told him we could call on his dead relatives, family members, and angels to come and get him.

I could see him getting into his Cadillac. Then his dead relatives came to meet him, along with the angels of light. We said our good-byes. Then I saw him go up into the light with my spiritual eyes. When I did not sense him anymore, I knew that it was done. He was at peace and had arrived in the light. I knew he was going to be fine. After that, I never heard another dish rattle.

Exercise: Communicate with A Deceased Loved One

If you want to communicate with your deceased loved one, you can use a technique called etheric communication. Visualize your deceased loved one in front of you, and talk aloud to him or her. You can easily have a two-way conversation. Wait and listen for any thoughts that come into your mind. There is no reason to fear. He or she still has a personality and feels the same love toward you—there is only love, peace, and forgiveness once we go up into the light. Sometimes you may smell your deceased loved one's scent, especially if it is strong, like cologne or tobacco. Other times you will see pictures in your mind of that person doing something, or you will simply feel a presence around you. As you communicate, clearly imagine the other person is there. If they have not gone into the light, or even if they are evil, they will not be able to hurt you if you protect yourself and live in a higher frequency of love and light.

My Mother Calling My Name

My mother had recently passed on. I was at work, and all of a sudden, I heard my name being called. I looked around but did not see anybody. Then I recognized the voice—it was my mother's. She was calling my name and wanted help. I was going to fly to California to attend the funeral the next day; my mother was due to be cremated. All of a sudden, after hearing my name, I had a vision— with my eyes open. I could see my mother underground, in a building that was dark and completely made out of wood and stone. I saw her walking down a hallway. There were no doors or windows. It was like a holding place. I could not believe what I was seeing, in broad daylight and at work!

In my mind, I told her to go sit down on a bench I could see. I told her to wait there until I got home, and then I would help her. While I was talking to her, I looked at the wall to her right. There was screaming and yelling going on behind the wall. It sounded awful, like someone was being tortured. I thought to myself, "What is this? This is an awful place." I realized my mother was not behind that wall, though; she was in the empty hallway by herself, and that made me feel slightly better.

When I got home, I went into meditation. I found my way back to where she was sitting on the bench. I was told that a stairway would appear. All of a sudden, a spiral stairway appeared in the center of the hallway, out of nowhere. I was told by an angel to take my mother's hand and to lead her up the steps, but that she would have to think of a different quality of God to advance up each step. She needed to go to "the fifth level," the voice told me. Once she made it to the third level, the angels would escort her the rest of the way. It was up to me to take my mother's hand and to help her think of all these different qualities of God.

It was difficult for her, but she managed somehow to think of qualities such as love, peace, hope, trust, and purity as she continued up the stairs. I stayed with her until we got to the third level. Then the angels came and took her up to the fifth level. I could see houses, buildings, grass, and rainbows there. The angels mentioned that she would be okay. The stairway disappeared, and I found myself back in the present time, in meditation. I thought to myself, "I forgot to do something about the souls behind that wall that were screaming." When I had gone down to help my mother, I had no memory of that situation. I did not even think about it. I was told that I was not meant to help them, only my mother.

And Miss My Own Funeral

My father came to me after his death, in spirit form. Shortly after he died, I was driving to Phoenix from Sedona, where I lived. I was going to take an airplane to California to attend the funeral. I had the radio play-ing loud. I was by myself in the car, but all of a sudden, I felt a presence sitting beside me. Before I realized it was my father, he started speaking into my mind. It was unmistakably his voice and his personality. His voice was so loud that it shook me up, so I turned the radio down. I could not believe it was happening. I never really knew my father, had never been close to him. I never commu-nicated that much with him while he was alive, so I was surprised to find that he wanted to communicate with me after death. He told me that he could visit with me until I got to Phoenix, but then I would never hear from him again. He also told me how disoriented and confused he was. I told him he was dead and that he could go into the white light. He replied, "And miss my own funeral?"

I asked him, "Will you be going on the airplane with me?" He said, "It is bad enough that I have to sit through this luggage here in your car—I am not going to sit in another person's body on the airplane." I thought that was kind of a strange thing to say. However, when I did get on the airplane, I saw that it was completely booked, and there were not any empty seats. I knew my father liked to travel, and we did not yet know what time of day the funeral was going to be held. I told him to go travel around to wherever he wanted to go while he still had the chance. He was clearly planning to stay earthbound for a few days, until his funeral. Then he would go into the light on his own. The conversation was very interesting. I have to say that I feel that I got to know my father bet-ter after he died than I ever had when he was alive. He communicated many things to me that I did not know. I finally felt close to him. We talked for an hour and a half, until we got to Phoenix. Once we arrived, he said good-bye. I felt a tremendous love come over me. I started crying, and then he was gone.

I went to the funeral and felt nothing—I did not feel like he was there. We took a few roses from the funeral arrangements and put them in a vase of water. I took another stem and placed it on the dresser, without water. After four days, my mother remarked that the rose was just as fresh looking as it had been the day of the funeral. She could not believe it, and thought it was a miracle, especially since the roses in the water had wilted. I took the rose back to Arizona, and it stayed fresh. After about two weeks, it dried up suddenly. The message came to me then that I was to throw it away and release my father, so I did.

Experiences with the Deceased

When I was initiated into Reiki, level one, one of my spirit guides was Max, my cat. When I was initiated into Reiki level two, I smelled peppermint. My mother always chewed on peppermint, so I knew she was there at my second initiation. (Dina)

Her First Child

My grandmother died before I gave birth to my first child. I was very upset because I had really wanted them to meet. I cried and cried about it. One night my grandmother came to me in a dream. She told me to stop crying. She said, "I was there when your child was born, and I've been watching the child grow up. I am with you every day." I was so happy. I knew that my grandmother was okay and was with us. She came back to visit me. (Michele)

The Accident

I was driving down the road when I came upon an accident. I noticed that the woman in the car had been injured pretty badly. The paramedics had already come, but as I drove by the accident, I started praying for the woman. A couple of months later, I got a phone call. The woman on the other end of the phone asked me, "A couple months ago, were you driving by an accident where you prayed for the person in the car that was injured?" I replied, "Yes, how do you know that?"

The woman said, "I was the one in the car. I was dying, and for a moment, I left my body. I saw your car and your license plate number as I was floating up in the air. I saw you, and then I saw these flaming words coming toward me—a prayer. I followed the words down and could see that they were coming from your car and you. The words pulled me back down and into my body. I went back into my body and became aware that the paramedics were working on me. They took me to the hospital, and I recovered. I have friends at the DMV, so I got your name and number from your license plate. I wanted to call you and thank you." (Janet)

A Deceased Loved One's Perspective

"When I arrived on the other side after dying, I became very sensitive and open. My thoughts and feelings instantly became reality. I was manifesting everything I was thinking. Everything that was appearing to me was the result of my own thinking. I realized I had to learn to control my thoughts and not just react to what I was seeing. On the physical plane, it takes a long time for thoughts to manifest. Now I am able to think where I want to be, and I will be there instantly. I can travel by thinking of a destination, or seeing and communicating with others who have died. I seem to have the same personality and habits that I had when I was alive. I have the same beliefs. I do not feel any limitations or pain. Transportation is thought. I can read other spirits' thoughts. I can create my own heaven or hell, based on my thoughts. It seems like I have all the psychic abilities that we talked about on Earth, when I was alive. I can feel the emotions of other peoples' thoughts. I can see people on Earth, including my loved ones. I can see their lives and what they are going through. I see the angels all around and spirit guides that are trying to bring information and guidance to the people that are still living."

"After I crossed over, beings of light came to me and took me into the light. Then I had my life review. We looked at my achievements and failures. I saw how my actions affected others. It is all love and forgiveness over here; it feels very good and peaceful. Jesus Christ was standing on the other side already waiting for me when I crossed over. There is nothing to be afraid of when you cross over and die. Once you cross over, there is no pain, limitation, or illness. My recommendation to the living is to focus on the spiritual life of meditation, spiritual growth, and spiritual development. As I looked over my past life on Earth, I could see and feel everything that had happened just as intensely as if it was all happening again. Now the angels, my Master teachers, and my spirit guides will decide if I learned all the lessons that I should have. They will determine what lessons should be in my next life as well. When I come back down to Earth, everything will be arranged, with opportunities given to me that will be for my soul's advancement. With my free will, I will decide on the details of the plan. Any test or trial is a test meant to help us uncover a spiritual solution to the problem. I will give myself many opportunities to develop as my soul experiences negative situations and adversity. It is as if I will be going back to school when I go back down to my next physical life. I will then learn new lessons and come back here to my true home on the other side." (Ethel Wade, my deceased grandmother.)

The Golden Body

I had a dream where I died. I was with a couple of other people, a man and a woman. We were at a wellness center. Everybody was visiting, eating, drinking, and generally enjoying one another's company. There was a volcano nearby, and it began to erupt. The three of us were standing there with our backs to the erupting volcano. We knew we were going to die. We realized that we could not escape the erupting volcano; we would not have enough time to get away. The other people at the center did not know anything was happening, or somehow did not really care. All of a sudden, the heat of the volcano hit us like a wall of burning heat flame. It hit us so fast that our bodies were instantly incinerated. We immediately became spiritual beings. I looked down at myself and saw that I had adopted a transparent, golden body. I realized I had died and thought to myself how easy dying really was. I

felt good and peaceful, and I did not have any pain. I had
made the transition, and I was okay. After that, I realized
I did not have to be afraid of death.

The Spiraling, Sparkling Blue-White Light

I was awakened in the middle of the night. A celestial being
appeared to me in a sparkling, spiraling blue-white light.
The light kept going around and around, getting bigger
until it filled my bedroom completely. It was about three in
the morning, and it was very dark in my room. This blue-
white light was so brilliant and beautiful, appearing from
another dimension. I could not believe what I was seeing.
When I lived in Sedona, I had regularly gone to hear this
Master teach every week, but I had not been to the meeting for a couple of weeks. This blue-white sparkling light
swirled around for about twenty minutes. I was so surprised.
I nearly went into shock. This happened in 1995 when I did
not have a smart phone, so I could not take any pictures.
However, at the center of this sparkling blue-white light, I
saw this Master's face. I asked, "Who are you, and what is
the message?" I started to bow down in respect, humbling
myself to the being who was appearing in spiritual form
within a different dimension. I heard this message in my
mind: "No, do not bow down to me; I need to bow to you."

I thought that was very strange. Why would he want
to bow down to me except that the God is within me that
he was recognizing. After that experience, I went back to
the meeting. They told me he had died about a week ago.
"When?" I asked. "Last Wednesday."

I had seen the sparkling, spiraling blue-white light
at the time when he died. I believe he came back to

encourage me to continue on the spiritual path to enlightenment.

Manifesting Apports

What are apports? They are objects, manifested by spirits on the other side, which move from one dimension into another. I went to a spiritualist church in San Francisco years ago. They had different colored gemstones called apports. These had been teleported from a different dimension into the church. Some had manifested right out of thin air. The church kept quite a few of them in a large glass case, all kinds of different colors, sizes and shapes. The energy and power I felt when I looked at them was incredible. Each apport had a different quality. Whenever the church would channel spirits of deceased loved ones, more gemstones would manifest. The deceased brought them to certain people during the service. I would not have believed this could happen, but I saw it with my own eyes.

One of the men asked whether he could come visit me and bring a couple apports. He would offer to let me hold them so I could experience the energy of them. I agreed, and we met at the Rose Garden in San Jose. He brought two apports with him. The gemstones were both pink, but two different sizes. One was a transparent, faceted, pear-cut stone, and the other was translucent but also pear cut. I am not sure what they were made of. They appeared to be glasslike. They were an inch or an inch and a half long. He was carrying them around with him as though it was no big deal. He let me hold one; the energy that radiated from that stone felt like pure, unconditional love around me. It was very intense. I had never felt such powerful love in my entire life.

I was told that it was commonplace for these gemstones to appear out of nowhere during church services. They must have had thirty to forty of them in the case. Each one had a quality of God, such as love, joy, or peace. They radiated with a particular energy. They were like gifts from the deceased, from another dimension.

Pat's Transition to the Other Side

I once suddenly developed severe pain in my back and shoulders. I did not understand at first why or how I could have developed a severe pain like that. I found out the next day that Pat, a friend of mine, had died at around the same time I had first felt the pain. It had lasted for about four hours, and then went away. I realized that I was an empath and that subconsciously I had been helping her cross over and transition to the other side. Once she died the pain in my neck and shoulders disappeared.

During that period in my life, I began to realize a pattern was developing. I would take on people's pain and emotions and channel them into my body to help them as they crossed over to the other side. I rather adopted their pain. The angels taught me how to protect myself and clear my aura so I would not be drained of energy. Once I listened to the angels and applied the techniques for protection, I stopped taking on other people's pain. I realized I had been taking on energies that were not my own. The energies of others are not necessarily compatible with ours, so the result is that they can create blocks and pain in our body. This is another reason why it is important that we ground and protect ourself and keep our aura cleaned out. By sending the excess energy down through our grounding cord to the center of the earth and releasing it, we will be able to keep our aura strong and healthy. Too much energy in the body can create an imbalance and pain.

We must realize that we are energy antennas. We draw energy to us wherever we go—both from situations and from other people. As we release all excess and foreign energy, pain, illness, and stress into the center of the earth, it will be transformed into positive, loving energy. Then we will maintain balance and peace within our own aura and our life.

Sending Your Deceased Loved Ones Into the Light

* Ask your deceased loved one why he or she is still around.
* Convince your deceased loved one that he or she is dead, and that it is time to go into the light and be at peace. Affirm that God is all loving and forgiving.
* Call on your deceased loved one's dead relatives to come and serve as escorts. Then call on the angels of the light to come and assist as well. Call on Archangel Azrael to take the deceased into the light. He is an angel of light, a good angel. You can trust him to guide your deceased loved one into the light.
* Explain to your deceased loved one how to go into the light. Tell him or her to look up at the light, to greet dead relatives who have come as escorts, and

to go into the tunnel when it appears. If your loved one sees a dark cloud, have him or her go beyond it and there will be light on the other side. Encourage your deceased loved one to move towards the light and choose the means of transportation to go up in: on a horse, in a car, or on an airplane are valid ideas! Each situation will be different.

* Visualize your deceased loved one getting into the vehicle and going up into the light. A tunnel may appear at this point. Have your deceased loved one go into the tunnel. There will be a light at the end. As he or she goes into the light, the tunnel will disappear. Your deceased loved one will be greeted by a light being and will be taken to the appropriate level for his or her spiritual consciousness.

* Once your deceased loved one has gone into the light, you will sense it and feel peace. You will know that the transition is complete when you are no longer able to communicate.

Summary

We must realize that our deceased loved ones are around us and can hear us. They watch us, send us love and comfort, and point us in the right direction to achieve our purpose in life. Many come back as our spirit guides to help us. There may be times where you feel that your deceased loved ones are not around you, but as you call on them, they will come. Usually they will communicate with you through your dreams.

It is good to prepare yourself for your own transition by doing service and sending healing and love to everything around you. This will prepare you to have a positive mindset when you die and cross over.

It is also important after you die not to call for just anyone to help you, but be specific in who you ask to come assist you and take you up into the light. Call on either Jesus Christ, Archangel Michael, or your guru to come, assist you, and take you into the light. Also, give permission for your Guardian Angel to protect you during the process of going into the light. If the light appears to you step into it. It is possible after you die that an angel will appear to you with black eyes. Do not trust this angel for it is not what it appears to be. It looks like a regular angel, but it has changed its form into an angel of light. It is a fallen dark angel. Do not go with this angel, but call on Archangel Michael to come and take you into the light. Archangel Michael should verify any angel that appears to you after death, that it is a true angel of God and not a fallen angel. The fallen angel will disguise itself as an angel of light, and want to take you to a place that is not of the light. Say no and do not follow this fallen angel. Remember to call on Archangel Michael, Jesus Christ or a higher being of light that you are familiar with and know to take you into the light.

What spiritual practices can you do now to improve your spiritual growth and development?   List some ideas here.

1. _____
2. _____
3. _____
4. _____
5. _____

CHAPTER 12

RESPONDING TO OTHER-DIMENSIONAL BEINGS

———————

Ye are of God, little children, and have
overcome them: because greater is he that
is in you, than he that is in the world.

—1 JOHN 4:4 KJV

In the last chapter, we talked about how to recognize when your deceased loved ones are with you, how to communicate with them, and how to send them into the light. In this chapter, we will explore other-dimensional beings, UFOs, and biological entities. We also will discuss portals, going back in time, and the unexplained.

Have you seen a UFO? They can be different shapes and sizes. Different types of extraterrestrial beings simply have different types of spacecraft. Some of these ships are interdimensional and will appear out of nowhere in the sky, then disappear into another dimension just as quickly. We must realize that interdimensional beings have powers that seem supernatural to us. Many of these beings can communicate telepathically. Most of them look different from us because their home planets have different atmospheres.

My First Sighting

I went on a vacation to Sedona in 1992. I was driving from there with a friend up to Flagstaff, which is about forty-five minutes away. It was the middle of the day. We saw a UFO over the freeway above us. It was a saucer-type ship, silver, about the length of five cars. A cloud covered about half of it. It stayed there for about fifteen minutes, hovering. Then it was simply gone. I could not believe what I had just seen. It was my first sighting. I did not know anything about UFOs or alien beings at that time. I had never even read a book on the subject.

First Alien Contact

About a month after that vacation in 1992, I decided to move to Sedona. The morning after my first night there, I woke up and felt something in my left cheek. It had appeared there overnight. I also noticed a mark on the left-hand side of my neck. After wondering about it for many years, I have decided it is some sort of implant.

A couple of months after that event, I woke up at three in the morning. An alien was standing there, looking through my art supplies. I did not know anything about extraterrestrials then, so I was in complete shock. It had long arms, and they were moving up and down as they went through the supplies in the corner of my room. Within about thirty seconds, he disappeared. He must have been about seven feet tall, and had a large, diamond-shaped head. His arms reached down past his knees, to about halfway down the calves of his legs. He was tan colored and very slender—almost bony. When I saw him, I felt he gave off an aura of good energy, so I was not afraid of him. I had placed a yellow calcite pyramid in the corner of the room by the art supplies, so I thought he might have come to investigate the energy coming from the pyramid.

The following week, I woke up again at about three in the morning. A woman in glowing white garments appeared before my eyes. She looked human and had short blond hair. She was also looking through my art supplies. A girlfriend from Phoenix was staying with me at the time. When I saw the woman, I turned to wake my friend in the other bed. The woman disappeared before my friend had a chance to see her. There was no actual communication with these beings—they only seemed to be interested in my art supplies. I had been beginning to engrave symbols and numbers on metal to create jewelry pieces fitted with gemstones at that time. I suppose it was possible they were interested in what I was creating. I felt this woman was also good, and I became curious why everyone thought my art supplies were so interesting!

My final visitation was a week later, again at around three in the morning. I woke up to see a short, four-foot-tall Gray being checking out my art supplies. I felt a very negative energy coming from him, so I quickly became afraid. He looked right at me. I said, "I command you in the name of Jesus Christ, you must leave." Instantly, he was gone. At that time, I did not know what a Gray being was. I had never read a book about the subject of extra-terrestrials or UFOs.

I now realize these experiences started happening after the implant was inserted into my cheek, through my neck. When I was waking up from sleep one day, I realized I felt paralyzed. In my mind, I saw an etheric spider web around me. Then I saw a needle a foot long being inserted into the back of my neck. The only thing I could do at this point was to say in my mind, "No! You're not going to do this to me!" Then I visualized myself pulling out the needle as it began to go into my neck. I said in my mind, "In the name of Jesus Christ, I command you to go away." At that point, the needle disappeared and I returned to feeling normal. All these experiences happened within just a few weeks after I moved to Sedona.

The Laser

While I was still living in Sedona, a friend from California came to visit. We were invited to a UFO lecture, and we decided to go. When it was over, the speaker invited us to go out to a restaurant for dinner. We went with her and enjoyed the conversation about UFOs. When we got home, we went promptly to sleep. I was awakened at around three-thirty in the morning by a laser beam as brilliant as the sun coming down through my bedroom ceiling. It was focused over my stomach. Then I saw in my mind a sterile white room like a laboratory with extra-terrestrial beings experimenting on humans. It was as if I was looking through a telescope into another dimension. This all happened within a few seconds. Being half-asleep, I rolled over and jumped up. My friend was still in the bed, lying there unaffected by the event. I ran into the living room, and the beam disappeared. Everything went back to normal. I told my friend about it later. We concluded that the lecturer had set us up to be abducted by her alien friends. When she left Sedona, everything got back to normal again.

Visualization is a real weapon against these beings and against being abducted. If you happen to find yourself paralyzed, visualize that you are completely back in your body and in your mind command any beings causing the paralysis to go away in Jesus Christ name. If you make a decision that you do not want to have anything to do with aliens, they will probably not bother you. Place the protection techniques around yourself and say a mantra remaining psychically detached. The key is not to focus on UFOs or alien beings—that serves as a sort of invitation to them. Try not to think of them, visualize them, or have anything in your house that represents them. If you do, you will attract them into your life. If they are negative extraterrestrials, you will need to command them to go in the name of Jesus Christ and by his authority and blood. Whatever you visualize in your mind as a weapon for combating an alien becomes real in their dimension.

The Interdimensional Beings

After about two years in Sedona, I moved to uptown Sedona, to an apartment on the second floor. I began to experience episodes with interdimensional beings there. I could see into their dimension, and I would just watch them, moving geometric forms back and forth in another dimension. They appeared to be up against the back wall of my bedroom. These beings were very small, just about an inch or two inches tall. Their psychic noise started keeping me awake, so I was angry with them because my sleep was being disturbed. I would get up, turn on the light, and tell them to shut up. On a physical level, of course there was no noise. On a psychic level, though, I was being disturbed night after night. I would try to talk to them and asked them to move their operation elsewhere, but nothing changed. I was losing a lot of sleep. It got to the point where I had to sleep in the living room. This went on for about three months.

One day, I went to visit a girlfriend. She told me that she had been having a relationship with a Gray alien being and that she was pregnant with his child. I thought she was crazy and I did not believe her story, but I kept that opinion to myself for the time being. I decided to talk to her about the situation with the interdimensional beings since she seemed to have experience with aliens. I asked her, "Is there any way you can ask your Gray friend to come and talk to these interdimensional beings, and tell them to move their operation elsewhere?" She told me she would talk to him and see what he could do. I thanked her and went home. Within twenty-four hours, the problem had been resolved. The interdimensional beings had moved on. I could not believe it.

I knew then that she was telling the truth. She really must have had a Gray alien friend. I went back to her and thanked her. I told her to thank her Gray friend as well. She told me he had said that the interdimensional beings had no idea they were disturbing or bothering anyone, since humans usually could not see them. They apologized for the disturbances. I was grateful that I could have a good night's sleep in my own bedroom once again. It turned out that her baby was taken from within her before full-term by the alien Gray beings.

The Man Who Never Blinked His Eyes

I worked at Planet Hollywood casino mall in a retail store for a while. A man came in and started talking to me, telling me a story about when he was sixteen years old. His father had worked at Area 51. He took him down to the underground base to show him around. When he got there, they injected him with something, and he lost consciousness. When he woke up, he found an implant in his arm. He did not know what had happened to him.

I noticed after talking to him for an hour and a half that he never blinked his eyes—not once. He let me feel the implant in his arm. I decided to ask him some questions. He did not seem to have any emotions, and when I asked him if that was the case, he confirmed it. I asked him whether he slept with his eyes open, and he said yes. Whatever they did to him made it so he could never blink his eyes. We kept talking for a while, and he wanted to give me his phone number and take me out. I was scared and not interested. I took his phone number, but after he left, I threw it away. I did not want to have anything to do with him. I had a friend who would drive to Area 51 at night and stay there until early morning, trying to see UFOs. She had asked me if I wanted to go several times before, and I would always say no. I just did not want to open that door.

The Ufo at Area 51

My friend Kathy would sometimes drive up to Area 51 with her two sons in the middle of the night, hoping to see a UFO. One evening, when they had parked on a road nearby, her two sons decided to get out of the car and walk around for a bit. One son was in his twenties; the other was a teenager. Kathy decided to stay in the car. Her sons had walked about a mile down the road when all of a sudden they saw a UFO fly overhead. It went over the car, engulfing it with a bluish-white light. The circular UFO had lights all around it of all different colors. Her sons started running back toward the car to see if their mother was okay. The UFO flew off before they reached her. They yelled at their mother, "Did you see that?" She had been asleep and missed the whole thing. Her sons were so excited about seeing a UFO but sad for their mother, who had been trying to see a UFO for a long time. After that, Kathy decided to drive home—the experience was a little too close for comfort after all.

The Ufo Closing Door in Las Vegas

I used to be in the habit of going to a fitness club after work for a swim. I worked late, and it was not unusual for me to be there at about one in the morning. One night I got into the Jacuzzi. After a few minutes, my legs were burning hot; I had to get out. I looked down at my legs and they were actually burned as if I had been in the sun. I went to the management and told them there was something wrong with the Jacuzzi. I showed them my legs. They said they would check it out. I left the athletic club, got in my car, and started to drive home. All of a sudden, I saw a brilliant golden light coming from a large rectangular door in the sky. As I looked up, I realized I could not see any stars. Then I realized it was because a UFO mothership was stretched across the entire sky, blotting it out. I was so amazed that I pulled over to the side of the road. The door started closing from the top, and a panel slid down until eventually the golden light disappeared, and it was black. I saw it take off after that. I could see the stars in the sky again. I often wonder if my legs being burned had a connection with the UFO experience. It seems like a strange coincidence.

The Open Portal

I had another experience with a portal. This one showed up in the corner of my bedroom. Interdimensional and extraterrestrial beings came through it regularly. I decided one day that I would close it. Since I can see into other dimensions, I knew I could close it by visualizing and commanding that it close. I told all the entities and extraterrestrial beings that they had to leave through the portal and go back to where they came from, because I was going to close the portal. I allowed them fifteen minutes to go back through, I closed it down. I wanted my bedroom to be a peaceful place, free from interdimensional interference!

After the portal closed, I sensed that there was still a being in the bedroom. I asked him why he was still there. He said, "You closed the portal and I didn't have time to get out." I told him I would open the portal again just long enough to allow him to go back through. I did, and he left. After that, there was no more activity in that bedroom.

Contact with an Orb

I learned about a man named Riley Martin who was abducted when he was a child. He continued to have alien encounters. I would talk to him on the phone, and he would tell me about his experiences. I was skeptical at first and did not believe some of his stories. He told me that he would tell an alien to come and visit me so I would believe him. He told me I would see and hear a sound that would be something not of this world, but that I should not be afraid. He said it would take up to seventy-two hours for this visitation and that it would come as an orb.

I told him go ahead. I waited, and by the third day, I had nearly forgotten about the arrangement. I was sitting on my bed, getting ready to go to sleep, when all of a sudden I heard this loud, electric, crackling sound. I immediately saw a small orb about an inch in diameter. It moved toward me until it touched my forehead. I started seeing different colors and felt an opening of consciousness. It happened so fast that it startled me. Then I remembered what Riley had said. After that experience, I definitely was a believer. When I talked to Riley again on the phone, I told him what happened. The experience showed me that interdimensional beings are real and do exist.

Interdimensional beings and aliens do travel into our dimension by orbs and break the sound barrier, which causes the noise I heard. You will often see orbs around crop circles and UFO ships. These orbs are of different frequencies and colors, and they are usually translucent.

Growing Pine Trees

I had a dream where I ascended into a spaceship and I was a guest. Alien beings were going to give me a tour of part of their ship. They told me to wait in a room that had wood paneling and wooden floors. It had benches in it, so I sat and waited. There were other human beings in the room as well.

The aliens eventually came and got me. They walked me through a hallway that passed a laboratory. I looked into the sterile, white room and saw human beings subjected to tests. The aliens told me that since I was their guest, I would not be subject to testing. We continued out into a large open area under a dome. Pine trees were growing there—a whole forest of them in what appeared to be a greenhouse. As I looked up toward the dome, I saw a rainbow. I asked my guide why they were growing all those trees. He said, "We may need to repopulate the pine trees." These aliens called themselves the Xyliers. I had never seen or heard of them before. I do not remember what they looked like. All I know is that I was their guest and they were giving me a tour of part of their ship. They said they would not hurt me. I do not remember all the details. I found myself back in that room with wood paneling and wooden floors, sitting on a bench. Then I found myself back in my bed at home. I was not afraid. I felt that these beings were of a higher consciousness and were far away from the Earth. They seem to be an unusual species, not commonly known.

The Egg-Shaped UFO

I went on vacation to Congress, Arizona, back in 2009. The population of the town is fewer than one hundred people. I stayed in a motel. One night, I looked up in the sky and I saw an egg-shaped UFO. It was moving very slowly across the sky, so I could make out some details. It was large, and I could see designs and lights on it. There was no one else around; I was by myself outside of my motel. It was around eight o'clock at night. I watched it for about an hour. It moved very slowly across the sky, up and down and around. I had never seen an egg-shaped UFO in my entire life. I finally got tired of watching it and went inside to bed.

Missing Time and Time Warps

I was driving home from a friend's when I came to the intersection of Rainbow Boulevard and Tropicana Avenue in Las Vegas. I traveled that same way three times a week after visiting my friend. I noticed something was very strange. There should have been a Walgreens and a gas station there, but they were gone and everything looked empty, like a desert. There were suddenly very few buildings. I looked at the street signs again to confirm where I was. I continued down Tropicana toward Jones Boulevard, where I lived at the time. I kept driving, and it seemed like it took forever to get to the next intersection, which should have been Torrey Pines. Then Jones, and then Decatur. I passed Torrey Pines, but when I got to the next intersection, I looked and it said Rainbow and Tropicana. I thought, "That's impossible...I just passed Rainbow and Tropicana about fifteen minutes ago. This can't be happening." The intersection looked normal again. The gas station and Walgreens were back, as were all the other buildings around. I decided I would drive back the way I had come to see if I could find another intersection of Rainbow and Tropicana, to prove myself wrong. I never did. I went home, and everything seemed to be normal. Then I looked at my watch—I had left my friend's house an hour and a half earlier, and normally it would only take fifteen minutes to drive home. Even with backtracking to find the other intersection, I had only added another twenty minutes to the trip. I was missing about an hour. I really believe I went back in time or perhaps into another dimension. I believe I could have been abducted because of missing time. I will never know.

Back in Time

At one other point in my life, I had felt that I traveled back in time. I was visiting Spokane, Washington, on a vacation. Walking around some shops, I came to an old, abandoned train station. It was a busy area, with cars parked all along the streets and people walking around. When I walked toward the abandoned train station, something changed. I found myself back in time. I looked around, but I did not see any cars parked anywhere. Where the paved road had been, there was only a dirt road. I was in a desert. The stores were gone, and the only thing I could see beside the train station was empty land for miles. The train station was active, though, and there were a few people milling around near it. It was definitely an earlier time. I started getting scared, figuring I must have walked into another dimension or a parallel time somehow. I was not sure what to do. I decided to walk back in the direction I had come. As I did, I found myself back in the present time. I was so relieved! I figured I must have walked through some kind of psychic portal. I also had missing time in this experience.

Have you ever had an experience like this, or ever found yourself missing time? Think back in your life, and make a list of any unusual spiritual experiences you have had with alien beings.

1. _____
2. _____
3. _____
4. _____
5. _____

Summary of Key Points

* Place protection around yourself every morning.
* Call on Archangel Michael to protect you and place a shield around you.
* Eliminate fear and anger, and recognize that some other-dimensional beings are friendly.
* Be psychically detached and without emotion when you encounter other-dimensional beings.
* Call on Jesus Christ name and authority to command the other-dimensional being to go back to where it came from.
* You have free will, so you can refuse to give other-dimensional beings permission to contact you.

* Plead the blood of Jesus Christ over yourself.
* Remember that visualization is a real weapon against these beings.
* Remove any pictures or symbols that are connected to aliens in your home.
* Do not think about or focus on aliens if you do not want to communicate with them or be bothered.

PART III

HEALING WITH THE ARCHANGELS

CHAPTER 13

BALANCING AND HEALING THE CHAKRAS FOR WELLNESS

Let the Angelic Host bring down the sacred fire of perfection, love, and harmony into all the chakras, dissolving all negativity and bringing wholeness to them all.

In the last chapter, we covered how to respond to other-dimensional beings, UFOs, and biological entities. We also explored portals, going back in time, and the unexplained. I mentioned key points to help you protect yourself if you are contacted by any of these types of beings. In this chapter, I will cover how to balance and heal the chakras for overall wellness in your life.

What are the Chakras?

The chakras are spiritual energy centers along the midline of the physical body that regulate the energies within our body affecting our organs. Energy channels along the spine connect the chakras. Each one is associated with a particular color and quality. We will be going over these in more detail within this chapter.

Why are the Chakras Important in Our Lives?

Each chakra governs a department of life for example, our physical survival, our desires, our personal power, our relationships, our creativity, our psychic sense, and our oneness with God. The first three chakras help us function on the physical plane; the fourth through the seventh chakras help us to relate to others and develop our spiritual life. When the chakras are in balance, we have a more balanced lifestyle. We do have other chakras above our head and below our feet. We will cover the seven main chakras within the body. I do want to mention that we have chakras at the bottom of our feet for grounding and to connect us to the earth energy. We also have hand chakras to allow healing energies from God to flow through us to heal people, situations, animals, and the Earth. It is recommended that the chakras of our feet and hands be cleansed and cleared on a regular basis. When walking our feet chakras do pick up negative energies that need clearing on a daily basis. It is important to wash your feet especially underneath and to leave your shoes by the door. This will clear out negativity. I also want to mention that the hand chakras pick up other people's energy and negative energy as we use our hands throughout the day. It is important to wash your hands on a regular basis to cleanse and clear out negativity.

What Each Chakra Represents and its Purpose in Our Life

The First Chakra (known as the Root or Base Chakra) is located at the base of the spine for men and in the pelvic area for women. This chakra represents physical survival and how we function on the physical plane. It represents our physical health, courage, grounding, and vitality. The color is red, and the gemstones are ruby, red jasper, and garnet.

The Second Chakra (Sacral Chakra) is located below the navel and called the sacral chakra. It connects us to our feelings. It brings us enthusiasm, motivation, and energy to go after our goals. It is our creativity center and our sexual center. The color is orange, and the gemstones are carnelian and hessonite garnet.

The Third Chakra (Solar Plexus Chakra) is located above the belly button. It connects us to our ego, self-confidence, personal power, and mental clarity. It helps us with memory and brings us energy and inspiration. The color is yellow gold, and the gemstones are citrine, yellow topaz, and yellow calcite.

The Fourth Chakra (Heart Chakra) is located in the middle of the chest. It connects us to unconditional love, bringing forgiveness, compassion, self-love, and self-acceptance. The colors are pink and green, and the gemstones are watermelon tourmaline, aventurine, and pink sapphire.

The Fifth Chakra (Throat Chakra) is located in the throat area. It connects us to our self-expression, truth, and creativity. The color is sky-blue, and the gemstones are blue calcite, aquamarine, and blue topaz.

The Sixth Chakra (Brow Chakra) is located at the third eye. It connects us to our intuition and psychic abilities and removes anxiety and fear. The color is indigo, and the gemstones are sodalite and lapis lazuli.

The Seventh Chakra (Crown Chakra) is located at the top of the head. It is in tune with your spiritual self, wisdom, guidance, creativity, and oneness with God. The colors are white and purple, and the gemstone is clear quartz and amethyst.

What Each Color Means for Each Chakra

In the Root Chakra, the color is red, representing passion, energy, the feeling of safety, courage, strength, self-confidence, groundedness, and stability.

In the Sacral Chakra, the color is orange, representing passion, creativity, self-confidence, ambition, sexuality, laughter, and joyfulness.

In the Solar Plexus Chakra, the color is yellow, representing optimism, life force, energy, intelligence, happiness and self-confidence.

In the Heart Chakra, the color is green, representing harmony, healing, endurance, growth, peace, relaxation, and balance. The other color is pink, representing unconditional love for our self and others. Pink is good for anxiety, fear, and grief. It is also a youthful color.

In the Throat Chakra, the color is sky-blue, representing calmness, self-expression, clarity, creativity, and relaxation. It is a good antidote for stress and fear.

In the Brow Chakra, the color is indigo, representing protection, cleansing, and intuition.

In the Crown Chakra, the colors are white and purple. Purple represents psychic abilities, spiritual awareness, and inspiration. It is good for pain control and inflammation. The color white has rainbows within and is good for overall balance in healing, cleansing, and protection.

How do You Determine if Your Chakras are Out of Balance?

Chakra Questionnaire

Ask yourself these questions and see if your chakras are balanced or if they need work. Each chakra has a lesson we must learn while we reside in the physical body. We choose the lessons that we need to learn before our birth on the physical plane. Some chakras will be more out of balance than other chakras, depending on what lessons we need to learn. This questionnaire will help you determine which chakras are out of balance and need work. Once you finish, total up your yes answers. Then total up your no answers for each chakra. The yes answers show you are in tune to the qualities of that particular chakra. The no answers show you still have lessons to learn from that chakra.

Chakra 1: Root/Base

* Do you feel that you belong on this earth?
* Do you love and accept yourself and your body?
* Do you like to walk in nature?
* Do you like to exercise?
* Is your overall health good?
* Do you feel safe?
* Do you have a strong will to live?

Chakra 2: Sacral

* Are you able to express your feelings easily?
* Are you open to new viewpoints and opinions?
* Do you feel good about your sex life?
* Are you manifesting your dreams?
* Do you consider yourself a creative person?
* Do you enjoy arts and crafts?
* Do you feel motivated to achieve your goals?

Chakra 3: Solar Plexus

* Do you feel self-confident?
* Are you able to stand up for yourself and not feel intimidated by others?
* Are you able to set boundaries with others and say no to them?
* Do you have a strong stomach, allowing you to eat anything?
* Do you consider yourself a leader?

* Do you like things organized?
* Are you good at solving problems?

Chakra 4: Heart

* Are you able to give and receive love without fear?
* Are you an optimistic and cheerful person?
* Are your relationships satisfying and fulfilling?
* Is forgiving others easy for you?
* Do you accept others for who they are?
* Do you have compassion for others?
* Do you love and accept yourself?

Chakra 5: Throat

* Are you able to express who you really are?
* Do you see yourself as a creative person?
* Do you feel that people understand you most of the time?
* Are you able to stand up for yourself and share your opinion?
* Do you enjoy speaking to a group of people?
* Do you enjoy singing, dancing, or creating art?
* Do you love to communicate your ideas to others?

Chakra 6: Brow

* Do you see a vision for yourself to accomplish your goals and dreams?
* Do you have psychic abilities?

* Do you look at the whole picture?
* Are you able to visualize easily?
* Do you remember your dreams?
* Can you see a solution to your problem?
* Do you meditate and receive angelic guidance?
* Can you see into the future?
* Do you follow your intuition?

Chakra 7: Crown

* Do you feel connected to God or the universe?
* Are you open-minded and able to look at other options?
* Do you feel that you have a purpose in life to fulfill?
* Are you able to let go of the past and move forward?
* Can you see the big picture in your own life?
* Are you able to let go of relationships?
* Are you able to free yourself from addictions or people that are not good for you?
* Do you have compassion for all people?
* Do you love humanity and want to serve them?

Now add up the total yes answers for each chakra and the no answers for each chakra.

Root Chakra	Total yes _____	Total no _____
Sacral Chakra	Total yes _____	Total no _____
Solar Plexus Chakra	Total yes _____	Total no _____
Heart Chakra	Total yes _____	Total no _____

Throat Chakra	Total yes _____	Total no _____
Brow Chakra	Total yes _____	Total no _____
Crown Chakra	Total yes _____	Total no _____

Now look at your totals and see which chakras have the highest yes numbers. These are strong and you have mastered the lessons of these chakras. Now look at the no numbers, which show the weaker energy chakras. You still have lessons to learn from these.

Symptoms of Chakras When Out of Balance

If the Root Chakra is out of balance, you will feel that you are not safe or protected, and you will not feel grounded in your body. You may feel tired and not have a strong will to live. Your survival instincts will not be strong. You will not be able to manifest your goals or have a solid foundation. It will be hard for you to set goals and know what you really want in life. Addictions: alcohol and sex

If the Sacral Chakra is out of balance, you will not be able to express your emotions or feelings easily. You may have blocks when it comes to expressing your creativity. You may have difficulty in relationships concerning your emotional needs. Addictions: alcohol, food, and sugar

If the Solar Plexus Chakra is out of balance, you will have anxiety, fear, and digestive problems and will not be able to assert yourself or be independent. It will be hard for you to discipline yourself and have self-control. Addictions: food, caffeine, and compulsive cleaning

If the Heart Chakra is out of balance, you will be hesitant in receiving love and may not feel that you deserve it. You also may not accept or love yourself. You may not feel self-confident. Addictions: cigarettes and marijuana

If the Throat Chakra is out of balance, you may not be able to express your true self or communicate easily. You may feel not understood by others. Addictions: cigarettes

If the Brow Chakra is out of balance, you will have a hard time listening to your intuition and acting on it. It may be hard for you to receive divine guidance. You may become confused and fearful.

If the Crown Chakra is out of balance, you will feel anxiety and a lack of peace in your life. You will feel that you are separate not only from other people but from God also.

Lessons of the Chakras and Challenges

Root Chakra: The lesson is to be able to survive on the earth plane and have a safe place to live. To have physical safety, you must feel grounded, with food and your material needs met. This chakra represents knowing what direction you are to take in life. The lesson is to discover what you are supposed to do and what is expected of you. The lesson is to have the money to survive on the physical plane. What will it take you to survive on the physical plane to feel safe and grounded? Building a foundation of safety and having enough money to provide for your needs to survive on this material plane is connected to the root chakra.

Sacral Chakra: The lesson is to learn how to express your feelings of sexual love to another and how to receive love and pleasure. Developing a relationship and feeling emotionally safe in that relationship is also a part of this lesson.

Solar Plexus Chakra: The lesson is to develop self-esteem, self-discipline, self-respect, and independence. Standing alone, taking responsibility for yourself, fulfilling your purpose, owning your personal power, and not being intimidated by somebody else is also a part of this lesson.

Heart Chakra: The lesson is to give unconditional love and to be able to receive love from others. Included within this lesson is to forgive and accept yourself and others and to have compassion toward all.

Throat Chakra: The lesson is to be able to look at yourself honestly and to be able to communicate your truth and be yourself. It is all about asking for what you need and recognizing the choices that you have in life. Self-expression and being creative with the talents and abilities God has given you is included in this lesson.

Brow Chakra: The lesson is to be able to tune into your intuition and take action, believing that the information will guide you for your highest good. The lesson is that you will be able to trust the divine guidance coming to you from the angels for your highest good.

Crown Chakra: The lesson is to be able to become one with your higher self or Holy Christ self and bring this higher self into your personality. The lesson is to want to serve humanity with your gifts that you have and become one with the universal God through meditation and higher consciousness. This is how you will gain the wisdom you need to be able to serve others.

Activities You can do to Correct any Imbalances in Your Chakras

The Root Chakra is in tune with the adrenals, spinal column, bones, and legs. Walking in nature or doing exercise will strengthen this chakra. Visualize a brilliant red color, radiating within your root chakra. Any activity that will strengthen your legs or spinal column will benefit your first chakra and bring it into balance.

The Sacral Chakra is in tune with the reproductive organs, kidneys, and bladder. The activity you can do is to be creative, whether with the arts or with ideas in your mind. Another activity would be dancing or singing. These activities will help you to express your feelings and emotions, which will bring balance to this chakra.

The Solar Plexus Chakra is in tune with the pancreas, liver, stomach, gallbladder, muscles, and autonomic nervous system. The activity you can do is to assert your personal power while setting boundaries with other people and being able to say no to them. The other activity is to discipline yourself and learn self-control to bring balance within your life. If you can develop independence and self-sufficiency, you will be able to make the right decisions, choosing actions that benefit you rather than listening to other people who are trying to influence you. You will be able to stand up for yourself and stand on your own two feet. It is all about being able to use the power that you have in a constructive way to benefit all.

The Heart Chakra is in tune with the heart, thymus gland, circulation, lungs, arms, and hands. What brings this chakra into balance is the practice of giving unconditional love to others and yourself—and receiving love from others. If you can forgive the people from your past and have compassion, this will bring peace and harmony within your life. Remember to forgive yourself and love yourself; then you will be able to love others.

The Throat Chakra is in tune with the throat, neck, thyroid, parathyroid, hypothalamus, and mouth. The activity for bringing this chakra into balance is to speak your truth and communicate who you truly are to other people.

Honesty is important, and so is your creative expression, whether through art, speaking, or writing.

The Brow Chakra is in tune with the pituitary gland, ears, nose, and left eye. The activity for bringing this chakra into balance is to acknowledge your intuition and follow it. Be open to receive insights and clear seeing.

The Crown Chakra is in tune with the pineal gland, cerebral cortex, central nervous system, and right eye. The activity to balance this chakra is to love everybody unconditionally and realize that everyone is connected. Any judgment or criticism should be avoided.

Healing Affirmations from the Angels for Each Chakra for Strengthing and Balancing

Root Chakra Affirmations:

- I'm safe and secure and protected by God.
- I trust in God to provide for all my needs.
- I feel grounded and comfortable in my physical body.
- I am healthy and strong.

Sacral Chakra Affirmations:

- I am creative and full of enthusiasm, achieving my goals.
- I accept myself and express my feelings freely.

- I make the right decisions in life.
- I choose the right direction to fulfill my purpose in life.
- I am motivated and set goals to go after my dreams.

Solar Plexus Chakra Affirmations:

- I love and accept myself.
- I release myself from the limitations I have placed upon myself within my mind.
- I acknowledge my personal power and use it wisely for the benefit of all.
- I feel good about myself and full of energy.
- I set boundaries with others so I can do what I really want to do in life.

Heart Chakra Affirmations:

- I love and accept myself.
- I am worthy and deserve love.
- I love myself and others unconditionally and also receive love without fear.
- I tune into my heart to discover my passion and what I really want to do in life.

Throat Chakra Affirmations:

- I express my true feelings without fear.
- I express my true self and communicate clearly to others.

* I enjoy life while being creative and doing what I love to do.
* I'm honest with myself and others.

Brow Chakra Affirmations:

* I acknowledge my intuition and act on it.
* I listen to the angels, receiving divine guidance.
* I move toward my goals with purpose.
* I tune into my guidance through meditation.
* I develop clear seeing and discover my purpose in life.

Crown Chakra Affirmations:

* I am now living my dreams.
* I am one with God and the universe.
* I am now connecting myself to my higher self and higher consciousness.
* I am protected by God and the angels.
* Everything I need comes into my life with ease.

I hope you now have a better understanding of what the chakras are and what they represent. By determining which chakras are strong and which are weak, you will be able to focus on activities to strengthen the weaker chakras and bring balance among all the chakras within your body. You will feel more balanced, and everything will become more harmonious in your life. You will know which lessons you need to work on for healing and for your spiritual growth.

CHAPTER 14

HEALING WITH EMPOWERING THOUGHTS AND AFFIRMATIONS

———◆———

God has not given us the spirit of fear; but of power, and of love, and of a sound mind.

—*2 TIMOTHY 1:7 KJV*

In the last chapter, we covered balancing and healing the chakras. In this chapter, we will be covering a series of healing and empowerment thoughts and affirmations that you can use every day. These affirmations will uplift you, strengthen you, and point you in the right direction for taking positive actions and focusing on your spiritual growth.

Would you like to feel better about yourself and more positive about your life? By saying these affirmations daily, you will feel a lot stronger and more self-confident and be able to handle any kind of situation that comes up in your life.

1. The angels go before me and prepare the way to bring me a prosperous, harmonious, and peaceful day.

2. Everything I need comes to me in perfect timing with harmony and love.
3. I listen to my intuition and gut feelings as I go throughout my day.
4. I acknowledge that my Guardian Angel is watching over me and protecting me throughout the day.
5. The universe is friendly, and God directs me in the way I should go once I acknowledge Him.
6. The Master teachers and spirit guides bring me all the guidance I need to fulfill my purpose.
7. I call on Archangel Raphael to restore my body to health with his emerald-green light.
8. No weapon formed against me will prosper when I am walking in God's divine plan fulfilling my purpose.
9. God is all-powerful, loving, and forgiving; He can handle all my problems today.
10. I call on Saint Germain and give him permission to bring the violet flame into my situation to dissolve and clear out all negativity.
11. I call on Archangel Michael to dissolve all fear and worry and to cut me free from negative feelings such as anger and depression.
12. I send unconditional love from God through my heart, arms, and hands for healing.
13. As I operate from my heart and intuition, my life will become more harmonious, and all negativity will drop off and cease to affect me.
14. As I align myself with my higher self, I will be able to express love and serve others according to God's will.

15. Rather than reacting emotionally to what other people are saying, I will merely observe, then accept or reject what they have to say.
16. I work to become aware of my thought patterns every day so I can think about ways to achieve my goals.
17. I realize that thinking creates my reality in life, so I choose positive words and focus on what I really want.
18. I picture myself doing what I really want to do in life.
19. When negative thoughts come into my mind, I cancel them out and replace them with positive thoughts.
20. Fear is an illusion. I will step out even if I feel fear, going forward with baby steps and courage to achieve my goals.
21. I have choices in life and I am free to choose and make decisions that make me happy. I trust myself. I am taking the right actions and making the right decisions.
22. Every day I become stronger and healthier. I am full of energy and feel good.
23. My belief system creates my physical and emotional reality. To create new beliefs, I repeat affirmations and visualize the person I want to become.

I recommend that you say these affirmations daily. After you say them for a month, ask yourself how you feel about yourself and your life. I am sure you will be pleasantly surprised!

CHAPTER 15

HEALING EXERCISES FOR YOUR LIFE

———

For I will restore health unto thee, and I will
heal thee of thy wounds, saith the Lord.

—*JEREMIAH 30:17 KJV*

In the last chapter, I gave you a list of healing and empowerment affirmations that you can say every day. In this
chapter, I will discuss the spiritual cause of symptoms and
clearing them. I will give you an understanding of how
energy flows through our emotions and thoughts, and
how it manifests symptoms and illness. I will give you some
tools and exercises to enhance your well-being and health.

The spiritual causes of symptoms are rooted in the
spiritual realms. Everything is energy. Our patterns of
thought create emotions. Negative emotions are energy
and create symptoms in our body. If we focus on not feeling well or believe that we are sick, we can manifest that
reality for ourselves. Our ways of thinking can create negative thought forms that will affect us in a negative and
physical way. Our belief system has a lot to do with what is

going on in our life. As we become aware of our thinking patterns, we can change the way that we are thinking— and change our lives.

Releasing Negativity Exercise

Repeat the following: "I release all excess and foreign energy, all pain, illness, and stress into the center of the Earth to be transformed by Mother Earth into love, light, and blessing. I thank Mother Earth for her services."

Mother Earth is well able to transform negative energy into positive energy. She is also happy to do it.

Poison arrows, or negative thought forms, can also create physical symptoms in the body. They can create pains in the back and the knees that feel like arthritic conditions. Once we call on Archangel Michael to come and remove them with his magnet, the pain will go away or become less intense.

Spirit attachments can create symptoms such as pain, headaches, depression, and anger. Archangel Michael can remove spirit attachments with his large "vacuum tube" of the spirit. Just call on him and give him permission to do it. You can also call on the name and authority of Jesus Christ, and his blood, to remove spirit attachments yourself.

Any limiting beliefs that you may have can create problems in your own life—as well as physical symptoms. It is important for you to examine your belief systems and the way you think. Do you want to keep the belief systems you have, or do you want to create new ones? We tend to inherit and learn a lot of limiting beliefs during our childhood. Be sure to examine these ways of thinking, and decide if you want to keep them. You are giving parts of yourself away by accepting beliefs without questioning them. It is very important to have Archangel Michael cut the negative cords between you and the other person with his golden sword of the Spirit. Give him permission, and then visualize him doing it—believe and know that he is doing it for you.

Remember that the Archangels are here to help us in many ways, not only to cleanse your aura, but also to strengthen and heal it with their colored flames of healing and protection. Call on them and give them permission to work on your behalf. Archangel Michael will do the cleansing, and Archangel Raphael will bring the healing. These two Archangels work as a team and will seal up any tears, cracks, or holes in your aura. They will also fortify your aura with their green and blue light. Be sure to acknowledge the Archangels on a daily basis, and ask them for their help regularly. You will feel so much better physically and emotionally when you work with them.

Make sure to be patient with yourself, and love yourself. If you love and accept yourself as you are and believe in yourself, you will feel better about your life.

Nurture Your Inner Child: Loving and Accepting Yourself

Here is an exercise to help you nurture your inner child: by doing so, you will be bringing balance into your life. Place yourself in a relaxed state. Take a few deep breaths, close your eyes, and visualize yourself at a beach. You are looking out over the cliff at the water. Visualize a staircase cut into the cliff; take steps down one by one as you go deeper into relaxation. You find yourself on the beach a few moments later, walking on the sand and watching the waves roll in. Far off in the distance, you see a child playing alone. As you approach the child, you realize it is the younger you.

You walk over to and watch the child play with shells in the sand making a sand castle. You say hello and join in. Once the castle is finished, both of you look at each other and smile; you feel happy and joyful. You talk together, and hug each other, as if just realizing that you are family, and there is love between you. You stay for a while, continuing to talk and have fun. Listen to what the child has to say. Explain that everything will be all right. You will keep this child safe; you will take time off to play and have fun. The child is a part of you, and everything is all right now.

Merge with the child, and become one. Now that you are older, you can bring comfort and understanding to what happened in the past with forgiveness.

Walk back along the beach, watching the waves come in. Assure yourself that everything will be all right in your future. You have found your inner child within, and you have sustained him or her with love. Walk back up the stairs and return to the present time, finding yourself sitting in meditation and then opening your eyes. You should feel thankful, peaceful and happy.

Now that you have finished the meditation exercise, how do you feel about yourself? Say these affirmations:

1. I love and accept myself as I am. I believe in myself.
2. I make time to be with my inner child and have fun.

3. I choose to love myself and forgive myself.
4. I ask myself if an activity will enhance my self-esteem or diminish it.
5. I make decisions that are good for me.
6. I choose to accept and experience all of my emotions.
7. When I share my feelings and stand up for myself, I feel good about myself.
8. I let go of all my old beliefs and limitations that hold me back.
9. I value myself and am free to be who I am to be.
10. I always find my path and connect with the right people at the right time.
11. I am at the right place at the right time because I trust my intuition to guide me.
12. I overcome fear by releasing all my worries to God.
13. I let go and trust God to bring me what I need to experience spiritual growth.
14. God loves me unconditionally. My inner child is special to me. I acknowledge him or her daily.

You will feel so much better about yourself if you take time to meditate, think about your life and contemplate what you want. Taking care of your body is an important step in loving yourself and achieving your goals.

The Body Mind Connection.

How does your mind and your thoughts affect your body? How can you become a medical intuitive to your own body? In this section, we will cover a technique called voice dialogue where the part of the body will actually speak and channel through you to tell you what is going on with your body. The conference room technique represents the different parts of yourself and how they communicate their opinions about different problems and issues. Seeing into the body is a technique where you actually go into the body and adjust meters in the brain for different conditions. You may want to improve your eyesight, or adjust things within your body. You become a medical intuitive to your own body. You go into your different chakras clean them out so they are bright, shiny and clean. This will bring balance to your chakras and energy system.

Is there a body mind connection? I believe there is. Does your mind and your thinking affect your body and your health? I believe it does. A person must control his thinking and think positive to receive good health. Your thoughts affect your environment around you. You do create your own reality. Your attitudes, thinking, and emotions are all involved and interrelate within your energy system. You must change your beliefs within your subconscious mind to create a change in your health. Your beliefs, which are within the subconscious mind will be projected outside of you, and then back to you. It is important to recognize this.

Hypnotherapy, which is a relaxed state of mind, is a good tool to use to change a person's belief system. When your needs are not being fulfilled, the subconscious part of yourself will speak through the body with symptoms or illness. If these needs are not recognized a health crisis will occur. The crisis will get your attention to calm down and become aware of your desires and purpose. Then you will go within and receive guidance and information. As you listen to your desires and needs within, you can prevent many physical problems. The decisions and conflicts within your mind can bring disharmony and illness. Traumas and events are stored within your cell memories, and in the tissues of the body. These traumas and negative memories need to be paid attention to and will make themselves known as symptoms of the body. This creates a misalignment of energy within the body and inflexibility, limiting the range of emotional flexibility and physical flexibility. Emotions and beliefs are stored in the body. It is best to resolve any conflicts within the mind quickly and to be clear about the decision you are making. Be clear about your purpose in life and the direction you are going. This will prevent any injuries that may occur when you have prolonged the decision-making process and are confused. People express unresolved conflict, stress, frustration, and fear through disease and illness. When a person is fearful, pain is created within the body to alert the person of danger or not going down the right path. Memories and pictures within the mind will manifest pain or symptoms in the body. If a person pays attention to the pain they are having, they may be able to connect it to a stressful situation, or trauma that has occurred.

To clarify, decision-making, you can use a technique called the conference room. This is the place in meditation, where different parts of yourself are represented, seated around a table to give their point of view on whatever issue that is being discussed. The different parts of yourself include the judge, the rebel, the inner child, the priest, the task master, the rational mind, the heart, the body, the subconscious mind, the cynic, your higher self, your parents, or any other part of the personality. These different parts will sit around the conference table and discuss the issue by giving their opinions about it. Once the different parts of yourself come into an agreement and make a decision about whatever the issue is, peace, harmony and health will be restored. If you do this on a regular basis, you can prevent illness or injuries. You will understand yourself better if you practice this technique when you have to make a decision. Hypnotherapy deals with core emotional issues that are behind belief systems that a person has. These beliefs are hidden in the subconscious mind and in the cell memories. When a person goes through a hypnotherapy session he is able to access his beliefs within the subconscious mind and determine the thought patterns, and emotions connected to the belief system. Once the belief system is uncovered, a person can be healed. These limiting beliefs can be changed. As we grow up, we adopt these limiting beliefs of others, which are then reinforced by other situations in our life. These beliefs become strong and attract everything that is in agreement with them.

The Conference Room.

I will be talking about the conference room now where the person goes into meditation. You will go down a flight of stairs to a conference room to confront and negotiate the different parts of yourself, which are subpersonalities that have an opinion on your issue or problem. Before you go down to the conference room you need to choose an issue or problem that you are having in your personal life where there is a conflict within you. Your subconscious mind maybe thinking differently than your conscious mind about the problem or issue. You will walk into a room, and visualize it in your mind with different subpersonalities around the table. These are the different parts of yourself. You would ask each one to speak and give their opinion about the issue or problem at hand. Before you do that, look around the room and see which parts of yourself are there, seated at the table. Most likely the ones that would be in agreement with each other will be next to each other. Each part will have an opinion. Ask each one to speak and express their opinion on the issue at hand. Realize that you are the one in control of this group. They are all a part of you, but you are running the show. Do not let it get out of hand. You present the problem to them. Then you can ask each one their opinion on how to resolve the issue or problem. You give each one an opportunity to express their opinion about the problem. You must be in control because each one will want to talk a long time. You will have to tell each one now it is time for you to speak.

The purpose of the conference room is to have all the different parts of yourself negotiate and come to an agreement concerning the issue at hand to solve the problem. There is going to be conversations between the different parts of yourself. They will give you their points of view on how they would solve the problem. They will also express their desires and what they want and do not want. There may be a few subpersonalities or parts of yourself that are afraid. They will create symptoms throughout the body to try to get their message across. It is the only way they can be heard. I have experienced it in my own life. I work too hard and the inner child suffers because of it. The inner child wants to play and create art where the other part of me wants to work a lot. Within the conference room, I would have these two parts of myself have a conversation and come to an agreement to bring balance into my life. Then I would bring more fun into my life. The decisions are made by the agreement of all the parts concerned. All of them need to express their opinions and negotiate so they can reach an agreement concerning the decision that needs to be made. You can go into the conference room and find out what really is going on within yourself. What is causing you to have these habits? Why are you attracting certain people into your life? No matter what the problem is, it can be solved within the conference room. Is there a sub personality that wants to control everything? If you do not want to work, and you want to play all the time that means that the inner child has taken over. You need to go within and find out what is going on, so everything can be brought into balance. When things are out of balance, the health can be affected in a negative way. The symptoms can also represent the undeveloped parts of yourself that need to be strengthened and recognized.

Your Guardian Angel and inner healer can help you within the conference room. The inner healer can tell you about what is going on in your body and can recommend things you can do to increase your health. The inner healer will discuss diets, lifestyle, habits, emotional states or anything else that would affect your health. Then suggested recommended changes would be given for optimum health. The inner healer may recommend teas, herbs, colors, music, or gemstones to be worn to help the healing process.

Sometimes the soul will intervene and create an illness or accident so the person will discover talents and gifts that he needs to develop to serve humanity. This is the only way that the person will slow down and reevaluate his life and the direction he is going. Sometimes the soul will create a trauma or illness, which is karmic in nature to have the person learn a lesson, which is part of their purpose in this life. If the person is too independent, he may have to learn the lesson of depending on others for support or to work as a team with others.

Voice Dialogue

There is a technique that you can do to explore the meaning of the symptoms in your body. This technique is called voice dialogue. You ask the part of the body that is having the symptom questions and you will discover the meanings, the memories and images related to the symptoms. While in meditation, traumas and the memories within the body can be healed through this process. Voice dialogue is a technique where you talk to the part of the body, which has the symptoms. You ask the body to speak and to explain why there is pain or inflammation within the body. Talk to the part of the body as if it is a person. Find out how it is helping you by creating the symptom. Ask how it feels or thinks about what is going on. Communicating with the part of the body that has the symptom can be very helpful with self-destructive behaviors. Most often personal needs are not being fulfilled.

An example of voice dialogue, asking questions of the body: the lower back will speak: we are not being appreciated for the strength we have given this body. We have had to put up with low self-esteem. We have struggled to survive and maintain this body and the parts of the body do not seem to appreciate our efforts and are not interested. We should all be working as a team and communicate among ourselves to be strong. We need to be appreciated from the other parts of the body. We are determined to get our message across, for our flexibility. We lock up any area to get your attention. The request is now to love the body, and thank the body for support. This is an example of the lower back and its opinion through channeling. This helps us to understand what is going on with a particular part of the body. This message from the lower back, referred to stiffening and creating pain because it was not being appreciated or loved. This is one example of the lower back speaking.

Another example of the upper back speaking: we are heavy laden with guilt and burdens that are not ours to carry. You have made us carry them and have overworked us to the point of exhaustion. We are carrying burdens from the past. Every person that you have felt guilty about; his or her problems have been held in your upper back. You must release these people. Let go and forgive, and release the punishment of yourself for your actions that you have committed. You have taken all their energies and problems and have internalized them to heal them. You must release the pain and the energy that are related to them. We are not able to carry much more. Give the burdens to Jesus Christ. This is another example of the upper back, a part of the body communicating what is going on and how it feels about the situation. Be sure to love and appreciate your body. Be sure to forgive yourself and not punish yourself, or sabotage yourself. God has created you for a purpose. He wants you to love yourself and take care of your body. The body is important, and the temple of the Holy Spirit.

You can do this with any part of your body that is hurting or has a symptom. It will communicate with you. It is a very helpful technique to understand yourself and how you really feel inside.

Voice Dialogue/Communicating with the Body

Close your eyes and relax. Take a few deep breaths. Send your mind to the part of the body where you have a symptom. Visualize your attention on that area of the body. Talk to the part of the body where you have the symptom. Ask as if the part is a person. Ask the body, "Would you like to speak about how you feel? What are you trying to tell me? I give permission for this part of the body to speak."

Next, quiet your mind and listen to any thoughts that enter. Trust that the injured part of the body knows how to speak to you. You can write down or record whatever comes into your mind on a smartphone. After receiving the information, you can talk to the body and then respond to it with ideas about how you can fulfill its needs and concerns. After listening and responding to the part of the body that you are acknowledging, continue to ask it questions and find out what its needs really are. Once you understand that your lifestyle is preventing you from achieving what you really want in life, you will realize that the symptoms are there to give you a message: you need to harmonize and bring balance into your life again. Most likely, the symptoms are there to slow you down and make you reevaluate your decisions. Once you are done, bring yourself back. Open your eyes and come back into the room.

This is a good exercise because our lifestyles are so busy that we rarely take the time to get quiet or even to relax and have fun.

Seeing into the Body.

Seeing into the body is another technique, you can use. It is like being your own medical intuitive. It is clearing your chakras, cutting negative cords to other people, removing negative energy, limitations and armor around you that holds you back. As you work with Archangel Michael and Archangel Raphael you will be able to determine what is going on in your body as they clear, and heal it on an energetic level. Part of this technique involves meters within the brain to be adjusted to affect the functions of the body. You can go within the body through this technique and correct imbalances through visualization and intention. To help a persistent injury to heal, visualize a green ointment to place on the area, and a bandage inside the body. You can also place a green colored light on it to help the healing process. The blue color can also be used to calm inflammation.

Seeing into the Body Technique:

Close your eyes and see yourself getting smaller and smaller walking into your brain. You see different meters and a control panel. Each meter has a half circle and an arrow pointing up to the center of the half circle. You can move and point the arrow from zero to 10. You can adjust the arrow. Each meter can represent a different area of the body. For example, a meter can represent pain or discomfort within the body. You can move the arrow down to a number one, which would represent a slight discomfort. Then push the button to set it and lock it to the number one. With your intention, tell the arrow it cannot go above number one. Do this first and see how you feel as you do this exercise on a daily basis. Once you feel comfortable and see the effect where you feel better; then you can do the exercise and bring the arrow down to zero. Most people will be able to believe that their pain can become discomfort rather than being eliminated altogether. That is why we recommend that you set the meter arrow to number one rather than zero. When you go into the brain and you look at the meter for the pain level see where the arrow is. Look at the meter and the number of where the arrow is pointing. It will be from zero to 10. Then you will know you need to bring it down to a number one, push the button and lock it into that position. Now the setting has been locked to a number one. You do this, all through visualization within your mind. The meter can relate to anything. The meter can be used to lower blood pressure, improve eyesight, strengthen your immune system, have your thyroid work better or whatever you need within the body. You can also use a PA system to communicate and instruct the cells to function better and to increase the immune system, or to carry toxins out of the body. You can visualize a computer screen and type in the instructions that you want to communicate to the cells within your body. Be sure to call on the Archangels and your Guardian Angel to come assist you in this process.

As you see into the body, you may find armor around the body. You may ask, what is that? Sometimes we unconsciously put an armor around us to protect us on an energetic level from an attack of criticism or threat. We do not see it with our eyes. If you go into the body and look, intuitively, you will be able to see armor on different parts of the body. Ask to see any armor placed on your body. A lot of it comes from past lives. If you have any neck problems or shoulder pain it is most likely been triggered in this life from a past life trauma. The subconscious mind will place this armor over those areas that have been hurt, whether it be in this life or a past life. It is possible in a past life that the person was hanged or he had a metal device around his neck where he was tortured. There may be armor around the shoulder area, with screws holding it in place, which decreases flexibility and creates pain in the area. The armor gathers on the body as a protection device by the subconscious mind. You can remove it by going into the body and calling on Archangel Michael to assist with his tools to remove the armor. Go into meditation and see with your imagination and ask that you be shown this armor around the body. You will begin to sense it and intuitively see it. You can have armor on any area of the body. The armor can be on your feet, your wrists or anywhere constricting you. Archangel Michael will assist you with his tools by unscrewing the armor and removing it. You will be able to see that the armor is in different layers. After the removal of the armor, call on Archangel Raphael to come and spray the area, with a special disinfectant to remove any residue of negative painful energy. Then have him spray a green oil or place ointment to heal the areas. This will renew and bring the part of the body into normal functioning once again. After the removal of the armor you can continue to have it sprayed every day to lubricate the areas and keep them functioning well. This will clear out any residue and help the healing process. You can do this technique on a regular basis. If the problem returns, you need to go in and find out what the cause is on a spiritual level. To do this, you would go back into the body in a meditative state or communicate with the body. Find out if the condition or the armor is from a past life, or from this life and what traumas are connected to it. You can always go into the conference room, or do the voice dialogue technique and ask the body. Why are you allowing armor to be placed on you? The body will probably tell you it is a protection device because of fear and being afraid. Most of the time it is from a past life. Sometimes it can be from an abusive childhood. In this case, you would automatically protect yourself against any verbal, physical or mental abuse. Your subconscious mind would have placed up a wall of protection automatically in case that would ever happen again.

Past life connections can have an influence and create symptoms in the present life. A person's cell memories from a past life of being injured remain with him in this life and can be activated or triggered by certain events or situations. It has become a pattern from a past life that has been carried over to this life, which create symptoms within the body. To heal or change any traumatic event that you see or any negative patterns from a past life, you can picture the opposite. Then you can go back into a past life on your own to heal and change the traumatic events. You can visualize the traumatic experience you had in a past life and change it to how you want it. This is called changing events. Place a positive event in there and change it. You write the script or write the story of your past life, as you want it to be. That is how you change the cell memories within the body. All the traumatic events of negative thoughts are within you from life to life. This is the way to change and heal them. All the negative decisions that you made back in a past life create unresolved emotional, mental, and physical residue that has been brought to the present life and has affected your life now. Go back into the past life and see what the lessons were and what was the purpose back then? Call on Archangel Raziel to go with you and assist you in healing your memories and showing you the lessons of that past life.

Past life regression releases and heals negative emotions and the limiting decisions made in a past life. Issues that are clarified and resolved with love and forgiveness will bring healing around those events that were traumatic to you. This will reevaluate the events in time, and

create a new future for you. You need to see yourself forgiving and giving to others. Every time you go back to a
past life, it can be a different past life. You can learn from
the different past lives, seeing the memories, and pictur-
ing them in your mind what you wanted to have happen.
If you are having a problem, you can go back to a past
life, and ask what past life is connected to the problem
you are having in the present life. Then you take yourself
back to that past life, and it will be shown what happened
back then and the patterns that were carried over to your
present life that need to be healed. Visualize how you
want the pictures to be. You can visualize a relationship
and that it turned out wonderful in that situation. What
you are doing is rewriting the script of your past life. You
still need to know what you learned in that past life. Past
life regression reprograms all the beliefs and decisions
that you made back in a past life. The meaning that you
gave the traumatic event affects you in a certain way. If
you go back to a past life and change the meaning and
the pictures in your mind about that traumatic event, you
can heal it. Picture a positive outcome. It is the traumatic
event and emotion suppressed in a past life, which create difficulties in the present life. That is why we go back
into a past life. If you re-create your past, that will change
your present life in a beneficial way. Go back into a past
life as an observer so you do not immerse yourself into
the emotional negativity of the event. Rise above it and
look at it from above, so you can see what is really happening, and you can change the events. This is how you
heal the past. You change the meaning of the event when
you go back to the past life. Before doing another past

life regression decide what you want to heal, change or understand in your life; be specific about the situation related to the problem or issue. If any uncomfortable memories emerge, either change the meaning that you gave to the event or manipulate the scenario so it has a positive outcome. This is how you heal and work with past lives. These are some tips on past life regression.

The Health Wheel Exercise

Imagine a large pizza cut into eight slices. Each slice represents an area of your life. Think about each area of your life, and place a number from one to eight next to each slice. The number one should represent a small piece that does not get much attention. A larger number, close to eight, should represent a large piece of your life that is already receiving a lot of attention. For example, relationships, finances, spiritual life, health, career, relaxation, family, exercise, and diet would be areas to look at. Look at the areas again. What do you see? Are you giving more attention to some areas of life than other areas? You will discover that your life is unbalanced and will need some adjustment. You will have to alter your lifestyle. You can also use percentages from 10% to 100%. An area that receives a lot of attention would receive a 100%. This is a great visual tool to see what areas need to be worked on to bring harmony and balance into your life.

How Can We Send Healing?

Visualize white light all around you coming from the God source, so it goes through and around your body and then under your feet. Next, visualize the light coming down to the top of your head. It flows through you to your heart and then through your arms and in and out your hands for healing. Visualize light running through your hands and fingers. Direct the energy to heal a situation, person, or even the Earth. You are an instrument of God's love, light, and peace, so ask that the energy flow through you, and not from you. Continue to visualize this energy flowing to the person, situation, or area on the Earth that needs healing.

Different colors can be sent through you to send healing to different areas on the Earth. Remember that God does the healing, and be sure to give Him thanks. Ask yourself where you need to send blue, calming, peaceful energy. If you want to send healing to yourself, visualize yourself standing in front of you. Then visualize the green color of healing coming through your hands and direct it to yourself in front of you. Turn yourself around, and visualize your back. Continue to send healing to yourself.

Did you know you are able to send healing energies from God through you to any problem area on the Earth? Listen to your intuition and guides, and send healing wherever it is needed. Perhaps there is an earthquake area or volcanic area, and the blue healing energy is needed to calm the area down.

Ask yourself which situations in your life need healing energy. If you have financial problems, relationship problems, or health problems, send the green light to the problem or situation and surround it. Then release it— do not see it as a problem. Trust that it is taken care of right away. When a problem comes up, resolve it as best you can. If you cannot resolve the problem on your own, release it to the universe. Let God take care of it. Let it go, and then forget about it. Put it up on a shelf in your mind, so to speak, and focus on other issues. It should resolve on its own. The energy will go before you and make everything harmonious as you visualize and state your intention. Your intention is very important for creating and manifesting what you want in life, whether that means healing or something else. The power of God is within you and is very powerful for healing.

Healing the Etheric Grid on the Earth

What is the etheric grid? A system connects energetic gridlines, or ley lines, that create an energy field in and around the Earth. These ley lines are similar to meridians in the human body, where energy flows freely, and brings good health. If the energy does not flow freely along these gridlines, or there is an interruption in the energy, then problems and negativity can occur on the Earth. Negative forces come in where these ley lines are not strong. A battle is between the negative and the positive forces, using the energy of the gridlines of the earth. Vortexes and sacred sites are points where great energy is coming up from the earth, and these gridlines cross over each other. These vortexes become portals for other dimensions and other dimensional beings to travel in. They come and go through these portals and vortex areas. These other-dimensional beings can have good or bad intentions toward the human race.

If you want to help bring healing and peace to the Earth, I would suggest starting by working with the etheric gridlines. How does one send spiritual healing to the Earth's etheric grid system? The Earth's etheric gridlines or ley lines can be bunched up and need untangling and smoothing out. They also need to be strengthened, reinforced, realigned, and balanced. Some of the gridlines are very weak or are broken on an energy level. For healing purposes, we can send white-light energy to these gridlines to repair them. Wherever energy builds up, earthquakes and volcanic eruptions can occur. This is why we must smooth out this energy. To do this, visualize the afflicted area, and move your hands over the area, as if you are smoothing it out over the Earth. You will be told what areas need smoothing out as you send calming, blue healing light. You can also do this work to prevent earthquakes and to calm down areas on the Earth. Green energy can be sent to areas on the Earth for healing, and blue energy can be sent to calm active volcanoes or areas that are prone to earthquakes. Violet can be used to clear out negativity and transmute it into positive and loving energy. As you work, you will be told what color to use and where to direct this healing energy on the Earth. Count from 10 percent up to 100 percent, and then you will know it is done. You will simply feel and know when it is done.

In this chapter, I covered some healing exercises you can do not only to release negative energy but also to get in touch with your inner child to love and accept yourself. I also covered how to understand and communicate with your physical symptoms so you can heal yourself. I discussed the conference room where you discover the different parts of yourself expressing their opinions about an issue or problem you may have. We also talked about seeing into the body, adjusting meters and removing armor from the body. The health wheel was presented in an exercise to show you what should be worked on to balance your lifestyle. I mentioned how to send healing to yourself, people, situations, and the Earth. As you complete these healing exercises, you will find that you will feel better about yourself and your life. I encourage you to put these healing tools into practice and feel the difference.

PUTTING IT ALL TOGETHER AND APPLYING WHAT YOU HAVE LEARNED.

Now that you have finished this book, what actions are you going to take? I encourage you to place protection techniques around yourself every morning, to ground yourself, and to run energy. Be sure to place the white light bubble of the Holy Spirit around you, and then surround that with purple light, and finally surround both with blue light. Talk to your Guardian Angel and give him permission to bring you whatever guidance you will need for that day. As you place the protection around yourself every morning and talk to God and the angels, you will become more adept at knowing what you are to do each day.

Practice meditation or at least take time each day to quiet your mind and relax yourself. Contact your Guardian Angel so you can communicate and receive guidance on a daily basis; I like to do this each morning. Once it becomes a habit, you will start calming down and receiving divine guidance easily. After you have built up this foundation of protection and communication with your Guardian Angel, you can start working with

Archangel Michael and Archangel Raphael in different situations. Be sure to call on the Archangels and give them permission to assist you in your situation. Once you are used to working with the Archangels, then you can begin to practice spiritual warfare techniques in your everyday life. You will be able to clear out a room or office of negativity with the white light and the violet flame.

As you get used to working with the spiritual realms, you will be able to bind spirits in Jesus Christ name and authority, and have Archangel Michael take them away. Any spirits or ghosts in your home will be cleared by using the techniques you have learned in this book. As you begin to practice calling on Archangel Michael each day to cut you free from negative cords and negative thought forms, it will become a habit.

All problems on the physical plane have a spiritual cause. Everything originates in the spiritual realm; therefore, all problems in the spiritual realm will be corrected with spiritual warfare techniques. By now, you probably realize that the spiritual realm is more "real" than the physical world.

Once you begin to use the techniques of protection and spiritual warfare, you are preparing yourself to deal with any situation that may come up in your life. I believe the angels are all around us—all we have to do is acknowledge their presence. We can call on them to assist us in whatever we need. The angels are here to help us accomplish and complete our purpose according to God and His will. We will be able to overcome obstacles that are on our path with their help. Once you have begun communicating with your angels, you will be able to resolve issues and problems in your life better than you ever have before.

For the next thirty days, I challenge you to take action by practicing these techniques. You will discover the benefits of your Guardian Angel's guidance. The sooner you put what you have learned here into practice, the sooner you will see results in your life. You will see that your life runs more smoothly and harmoniously. You will feel better about yourself and stronger spiritually and physically.

Summary of Key Points

* Every day, place a protective bubble of white light around yourself and your aura. Then visualize the purple light over the bubble of white light, and layer blue light over the purple light. Then ground yourself attaching your grounding cord to the center of the Earth.
* Practice relaxing by stilling your mind through meditation. Take time to contact and talk with your Guardian Angel. Ask questions in the silence and listen for answers telepathically.
* Call in Archangel Michael, and give him permission to clear and fortify your aura with his tools of spiritual warfare. Ask him to protect and seal up any tears, cracks, or holes in your aura.
* Call on Archangel Raphael with his emerald-green light of healing and give him permission to restore your body to health.

* Practice clearing out a room with Saint Germain's violet flame. Always use the white light of the Holy Spirit first, then the violet flame. This will neutralize and transform all negative energy. After visualizing the violet flame filling the room, then visualize white light filling the room one more time.
* Call on Archangel Michael, and give him permission to protect you with his blue light as you go through your day.
* Ask the Holy Spirit to have you be at the right place at the right time so that you can connect with the right people according to God's will.
* Set up a daily routine that works for you to practice meditating, placing protection around yourself, grounding and running energy, and connecting and communicating with your Guardian Angel.

Summary of What You've Learned

* Protection techniques and how to ground and run energy
* How to contact and work with your Guardian Angel and the Archangels
* How to communicate and receive messages from your deceased loved ones
* How to send your deceased loved ones into the light
* How to tell the difference between angels, spirits, ghosts, deceased loved ones, and biological entities

* How to respond to each type of spirit, if contacted
* How to use spiritual warfare tools and work with Archangel Michael to clear your aura and home
* How to bring healing with the help of the Archangels

Now that you have read this book, I strongly encourage you to reach out to me with your questions, stories, or experiences with angels, spirits, ghosts, deceased loved ones, and biological entities. I would like to help you apply techniques of protection, spiritual warfare, and working with the angels in your everyday life. I would like you to e-mail me and tell me what you are facing concerning obstacles in your life right now. I wish you all good luck and prosperity in life.

Your Friend,

Dr. Virginia Wade

ABOUT THE AUTHOR

Virginia Wade, Msc.D. is an author, professional speaker, metaphysician, and hypnotherapist. She received her doctorate in metaphysics in 2005 from the University of Metaphysics, which is now the University of Sedona. She holds a BA degree in art and health education from San Jose State University. She holds certificates in timeline therapy, NLP, and hypnotherapy. She specializes in pain management techniques. For more than twenty years, she has studied crystals and gemstone healing, holistic health, and Vedic astrology.

After moving to Sedona, Arizona, in 1992, she started encountering other-dimensional beings—the veil between this world and the other side is very thin in Sedona being a vortex area. She quickly learned how to identify and respond to different types of other-dimensional beings, spirits, ghosts, and biological entities. Her psychic abilities opened up while living in Sedona. She moved to Las Vegas in 1998. At the same time, she became aware of her psychic talents for releasing ghosts and spirits from haunted houses. Communications from deceased loved ones always seem to find her. She is also able to communicate with and send deceased loved ones into the light. She works with the Archangels, specifically Archangel Michael, with his spiritual warfare techniques. She also works with Archangel Raphael when she focuses on angelic healing and pain management techniques. She offers sessions and workshops on Contacting Your Guardian Angel, Aura and Chakra Clearing with Archangel Michael, Crystal and Gemstone Healing, Vedic Astrology Charts, Quantum Healing Hypnosis/Past Life Regression, and Timeline Therapy. She currently lives in Las Vegas, Nevada.

BOOK VIRGINIA TO SPEAK
AT YOUR NEXT EVENT

———

Virginia offers Workshops and Sessions on:

- Contacting and Communicating with Your Guardian Angel
- Aura and Chakra Clearing and Healing with Archangel Michael And Archangel Raphael
- Clearing Spirits and Ghosts Out of Your Home and the Work Place
- Past-Life Regression/Quantum Healing Hypnosis Therapy
- Vedic Astrology Charts
- Pain Management Techniques/Hypnotherapy
- Timeline Travel/Creating Your Own Future
- Crystal and Gemstone Healing

Please contact Virginia for more information via e-mail:
quantumhealing222@yahoo.com
Mobile: 702-553-5467
www.opendoorswithin.com

www.ingramcontent.com/pod-product-compliance
Lightning Source LLC
Chambersburg PA
CBHW051944090426
42741CB00008B/1260